GROWING UP STUBBORN AT GOLD CREEK

By
Melody Erickson

Published by Vanessapress
Fairbanks, Alaska

©1990 by Melody Erickson
All rights revert to the author
Printed in the United States of America

No part of this book may be used or reproduced in any manner whatsoever without written permission, except in the case of brief quotations embodied in critical articles and reviews. For information address Vanessapress, P.O. Box 82761, Fairbanks, AK 99708.

ISBN: 0-940055-49-X
Library of Congress Catalog Card No: 90-071527

Book and Cover Design by Lisa A. Valore, Art • Design
Homestead map by Gay Erickson Prall
Railroad corridor map by Nancy van Veenen

Quote from *Spell of the Yukon* by Robert Service used with permission of the Putnam Publishing Group. ©1921 by G.P. Putnam's Sons.

ACKNOWLEDGMENTS

There are many persons to thank for help in the production of this book. The entire Vanessapress Board is fondly acknowledged with a special thanks to Lisa Valore and Betsy Hart for their technical and editorial expertise. My sister, Gay Prall, and my husband, Phil Deisher, also spent many hours holding my hand while the manuscript was being prepared for publication.

I also acknowledge the tenacity of all those fans who kept asking "When is the sequel to *Growing Up At Gold Creek—The Gonna People* going to be published?"

GROWING UP STUBBORN AT GOLD CREEK

To Mom and Dad—For the homestead years.

I wanted the gold, and I got it,
Came out with a fortune last fall,
Yet somehow life's not what I thought it,
And somehow the gold isn't all.

                Robert Service
                Spell of the Yukon

The author poses in front of Botner's house with the day's catch from the trapline. March 1966

ABOUT THE AUTHOR

There are times when all of us need to take care of unfinished business. *Growing Up Stubborn At Gold Creek* has been a piece of unfinished business for Melody since her first book, which was published in 1979. Since that first book, *Growing Up At Gold Creek — The Gonna People*, Melody has devoted much of her time to making a living, (something which has alway eluded her as a writer), pursuing family stability, and continuing her formal education. Melody has a degree in Journalism from the University of Alaska and is chipping away at an MBA. She has a feeling that by the time she gets it, the world will have as many MBA's as it does aspiring writers. Melody lives in Fairbanks, the black sheep of the homestead family, most of which chose to set down roots in Anchorage. She is married to Phil Deisher, a wonderful guy who has succeeded at making a living as a writer, and she is the mother of an equally wonderful seventeen year old daughter, Heather.

Melody promises not to write a sequel to this sequel...at least not right away.

Table of Contents

Introduction	9
Chapter 1 – The Gatekeepers	11
Chapter 2 – The Trappers	17
Chapter 3 – Whitey's Fault	23
Chapter 4 – If You Blink	29
Chapter 5 – Something's Rotten	37
Chapter 6 – The Hunt	45
Chapter 7 – Whitey Returns	48
Chapter 8 – To Catch a Beaver	53
Chapter 9 – In the Traces	57
Chapter 10 – A Real Thorn	63
Chapter 11 – The City	70
Chapter 12 – Changing of the Guard	76
Chapter 13 – Mr. Check–Um–Everything	81
Chapter 14 – Nick Botner	85
Chapter 15 – Stephan Lake	90
Chapter 16 – The Surprise	96
Chapter 17 – Death	101
Chapter 18 – Building Bridges	104

Chapter 19 – Close to Home	110
Chapter 20 – Fire!	114
Chapter 21 – The Waiting Game	119
Chapter 22 – Bearded Knight	126
Chapter 23 – The Seed	133
Chapter 24 – Old Ghosts	139
Chapter 25 – The View	146
Chapter 26 – Go Away Little Girl	149
Chapter 27 – Springtime	153
Chapter 28 – No More Land	156
Chapter 29 – When It Rains	162
Chapter 30 – Caught	171
Chapter 31 – Shouldering the Load	176
Chapter 32 – A Different Breed	183
Chapter 33 – John Returns	188
Chapter 34 – "Always Forwards, Never Backwards"	194
Epilogue	198
What Ever Happened to?	200

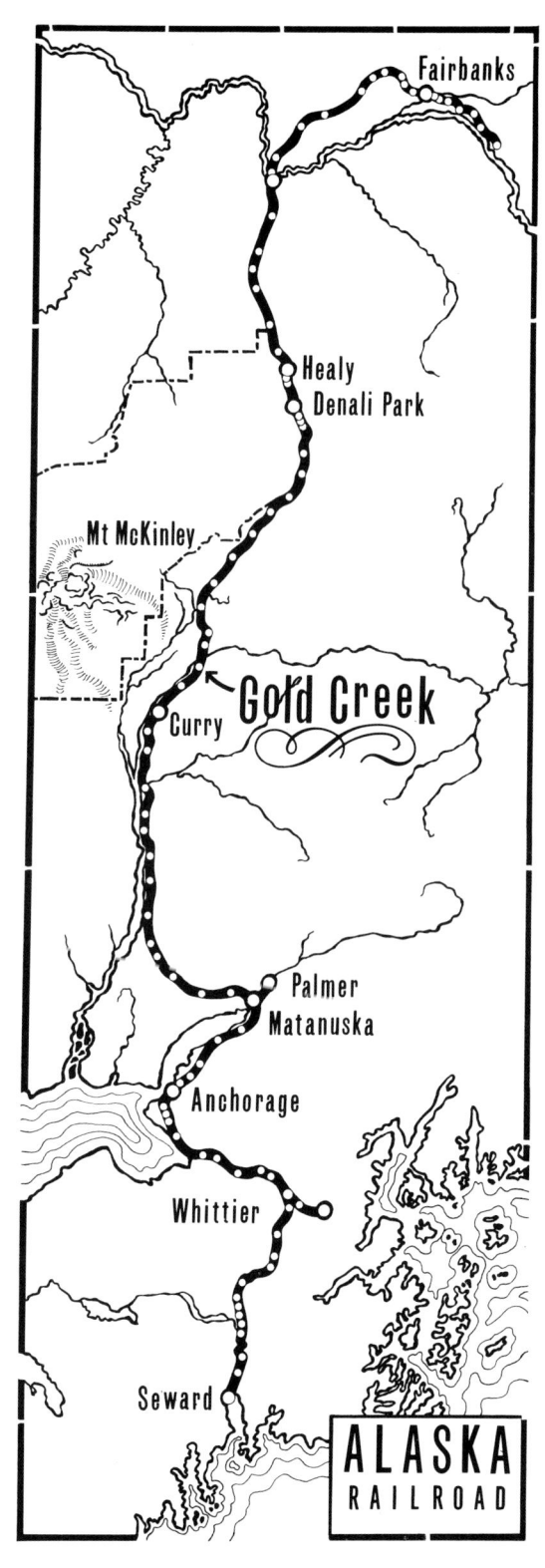

INTRODUCTION

There are times in everyone's life that are precious to them. Such are my experiences of homesteading in Alaska with my family. I was only ten years old when we pulled up stakes in San Francisco and cast our lot to the north. That first year at Gold Creek had turned us from newcomers, known as Cheechakos, into a family with a divided purpose. Part of us united to conquer the wilderness and meet its challenges, others longed for escape. But even as we struggled toward our own personal goals, the land shaped us.

I was the youngest and most malleable. I had sisters and a brother to study, sourdoughs, that rare breed of Alaskan mountain men, to learn from, and parents who mellowed as the years brought me closer to the end of my childhood. Sometimes I benefited at the expense of others. And sometimes I felt the burden of their failings. But as I look back now, I realize that most of all, I experienced the land.

This story begins where the first book I wrote, named *Growing Up At Gold Creek—The Gonna People*, ended. It continues to be a story about my family and their struggle to eke out an existence in the Alaskan wilderness during the 1960's. But, it is also a story of a young girl growing up, whether she wanted to or not.

CHAPTER 1
The Gatekeepers

I sat on the bank of a big spawning hole, waiting. Gay and Dad were in the kayak at the center of the large deep pool of water. My older sister kept the boat in balance with the double ended paddle while Dad stood at the bow with spear poised and ready. He thrust the heavy weapon downward. Water erupted in a brief struggle then Gay maneuvered the boat to shore where I removed the wiggling catch from the fish spear.

Fingers thrust deep into the salmon's gills, I dragged the heavy fish up the bank to our freshly cleared field. A late August sun warmed my back as I worked quickly with my sharp sideknife. Behind me the kayak slipped away from the bank of the first slough – a clear, quiet backwater that dumped into the nearby Big Susitna River.

Cleaning of the fish completed, I laid the fish with several others and stood, stretching my back muscles. The meadow in front of me looked strikingly different from the one I'd viewed the previous spring from the ridge–top where our cabin sat. The field's tall, waving wild brome grass and native fireweed was gone. Flat exposed earth stretched to the four corners of ten acres of freshly cleared land. The barren gray soil harmonized with ever increasing patches of russets and golds in birch trees. Several long piles of debris containing the overburden of virgin growth broke up the otherwise flat expanse. These windrows would keep our top soil from blowing away and give our crop of timothy grass a chance to sprout. As I stood, eyes squinted in an attempt make our grass grow, a scent more powerful than the smell of fish on my hands came on a sudden breeze. The musty odor of fermenting high bush cranberries announced fast approaching days of heavy frosted mornings, with brown leaves that crunched underfoot on trips to the outhouse. They were chilly, lively mornings, melted away by a full day's work of the sun as it passed over our valley in ever shorter arcs through an ocean blue Alaskan sky.

I looked forward to winter. John, my 12–year–old brother, and I planned to teach Princess, our Samoyed Husky and her offspring Panda how to pull a sled. This was the winter we were going to start our first trapline. I'd been listening to Whitey Rudder's every word all summer about the "how–tos" of trapping and was eager to put the sourdough's experience into practice.

A loud splash behind me cued the capture of another fish. I slid down the short, steep bank and waited in position to receive the next salmon.

"Easy now." Dad balanced from one foot to another in the kayak. "This one's a real fighter."

Gay paddled cautiously, anticipating Dad's moves as he tried to bring the large ivory–toothed red salmon to the surface. He stepped backwards, bracing a foot on the right hand side of the boat. Gay dug the paddle in deeply at the stern.

"I can't hold it," my sister shouted as the kayak listed to the right.

Dad tried to reposition, but instead lost balance and both fell head first into the clear, churning waters. Dad surfaced first, laughing as he clung to the side of the overturned kayak and helped Gay grab hold.

"I've still got him," he shouted. "Hang on. We'll kick into shore."

Gay grabbed the floating paddle on the way in and held one end of it out to me as they neared shore. I helped her out first, then both of us grabbed onto Dad's drenched shirt. We tugged him to shore where the three of us sat laughing while he pulled the spear towards us.

A large male salmon appeared tail first. Dad landed him on shore where the fish's unblinking eyes stared up at us. Claw marks on his broad side told of a near miss with a bear encountered somewhere along his journey home. I moved forward.

"Let him go." Dad leaned back, still catching his breath.

"We'll need that kind of spirit in his offspring. I'll bet that seven years from now all the eggs he fertilizes in this slough hatch and find their way back here from the open sea."

Careful to loosen the fish's tail with little damage, I nursed him back into the cold water. He remained still only a few seconds, green gill covers working rapidly. Then with a powerful stroke of his tail, the fish disappeared back into the deep.

There was no question of the salmon's survival. These creatures possessed what appeared to be a reckless abandonment of sense in their determination to obtain their instinctive goals. They would take a running swim through a bear's legs, a fishing net, or a falls on which they'd beat themselves again and again until exhaustion brought either success or death. I'd cleaned many a freshly caught salmon and held small pulsating hearts in the palm of my hand with a mixture of wonder and sadness. One time I'd even placed a freshly cleaned salmon in the water where it promptly swam away, and needed wading after.

"Let's call it a day." Dad used the spear to pull himself to his feet. "We've enough salmon for salting down anyhow. Besides, I can't take many more fights like that."

Gay and Dad helped me final wash our cleaned catch. Then we strung them on a long alder pole and carried the fish between us to the cabin.

"I wish I coulda been there." John looked out the cabin door to where Mom hung up Dad's wet clothes and laughed as Dad retold the story to her.

"It was a pretty stupid thing to do if you ask me." Sandra, my oldest sister, looked up from a text book.

"Well, no one asked you, did they?" I poured a cup of coffee from the can on the back of the wood stove. "Why is it every time Mom has a good time, you have to try to ruin it for her?"

"Leave her alone." Gay pulled on a pair of dry socks. She had just turned fourteen the past April and seemed to be taking more of Sandra's side lately. I was glad I had two more years before I became a teenager. But I promised myself I wouldn't act as boy crazy as Sandra. And I certainly wouldn't give Mom such a hard time over leaving the homestead like Sandra was doing.

"She's been a crab ever since Whitey took Doug up to his trapping cabin on Portage Creek." John fitted a newly shortened harness on Princess. "I think Sandra's afraid Doug is going to leave her here."

"He is not. We'll be married, no matter what Mom says."

"Then I'd stop dreaming and start studying if I were you." I sipped at the steaming contents of a mug. "Because that's the only way Mom's going to let you go…after you've finished high school."

"Let her try to stop me in less than two years when I'm eighteen. I'll be of legal age then and she won't be able to do a thing about it."

I picked my books up off a nearby shelf and placed them on the table in front of me with a loud thud. Gay jumped.

"Just shut up," she said, to no one in particular as I began flipping through the pages of a book.

Mom and Dad had ordered all our school books early so Sandra wouldn't have any excuse not to study. As a result, I'd dug right in with the seventh grade. Some of the material was already familiar to me because I'd sat right next to John the previous winter while he and Mom discussed the lessons. I covered those parts rapidly.

John and Gay hadn't tackled their lessons yet. Gay was starting the ninth grade and complained that courses from the University of Nebraska were more difficult than Calvert courses. Also, John was more willing to work outside, or go hunting and fishing than settle down to a textbook. We were less than a year different in actual age. So there was a time for ten days in November when I was as old as him. I paused in my studies now to watch him again try the reshaped harness on Princess. She stood still, a perfect model, as he marked the areas that needed adjusting with a red crayon. Panda sat nearby, watching.

"Don't worry, you're next, old girl," John talked to the pup.

She wagged her tail and nuzzled his ear. He pushed her away.

Somehow Princess and Ren's offspring didn't strike me as sled dog material. She was half Samoyed and half Sheltie. Almost full grown now, Panda was only two–thirds the height of her mother and had never lost her long silky fur and roly–poly body. In fact, she'd become rather broad. The pup was an overgrown lap dog at best, and when opportunity presented itself was usually in Dad's lap whether he wanted her or not, chewing on his ear.

This was a kind of thumb–sucking habit leftover from puppyhood when Princess wouldn't nurse her. Dad had sat up nights feeding "Little Darlin" with a milk–filled rubber glove. He'd then burp the pup over his shoulder, where she'd picked up the habit of suckling his ear. The cute trick had turned into an unbreakable show of affection to anyone who came near.

I looked back down at my text when Mom entered the cabin. She paused for a few seconds to let her eyes adjust to the dim light of the small twelve by twenty foot cabin.

"John, I think that's about enough time on those harnesses. You'd better bring out your school books. You too, Gay." Mom put some spare clothespins in a bucket near the sink. If we didn't take them off the line, the squirrels quickly claimed them, for reasons only a squirrel could know.

"I only have a little more to do." John worked quickly. "Whitey's dogs must have been a lot bigger than ours."

"All right. But I want to see you at those books no later than a half hour from now."

"Okay. Okay." John took the harness off. "It's not going to snow for awhile yet anyway. I've got plenty of time to do this."

"And I want to see a lesson completed by every one of you by tonight," Mom continued. "How about you Sandra?" Mom sidestepped Panda who had laid down in the middle of the cabin floor.

"I'll have a lesson ready to go on tonight's train."

"Along with a love letter to Doug." John fluttered his eyelids.

"So what if I do? It's none of your business."

I got up slowly from the table and headed for the door.

"Just where do you think you're going, Melody?" Mom stopped me.

"I'm going to help Dad salt the fish."

"Is your school lesson done?"

"Yes, ma'am." I met her eyes steadily.

"Okay, then. You can go."

John started to follow me.

"And where are you going?" I heard Mom challenge my brother as the door closed behind me.

Taking deep breaths of fresh fall air, I walked rapidly over to the log cabin we'd built that spring and used as a storage cabin. It had a roof so steep that Dad said it could split a raindrop. Mom nicknamed it the chalet, and the name had stuck. As I approached Dad, he continued to prepare the fish.

"How'd you spring free from schoolwork?" He looked up.

"I'm done for the day. But even if I weren't, I didn't want to stay inside. Mom and Sandra are about to go at it again."

Dad's brow furrowed deeply as he continued his work. I knelt near the barrel and helped layer the slabs of salmon and salt into the wooden keg in silence. Doug had asked for Sandra's hand in marriage that summer. She was sixteen years old and Mom said no. Since that time my oldest sister had been making certain that if she were "stuck in this hell–hole" and not allowed to have fun, no one else would have any fun either. I hoped Mom would change her mind and let Sandra go so we could have some peace in the family.

Suddenly tired of preparing fish, I stood up and walked the few feet to the chalet. The plank shelves bulged with home canned fish, meat, and mushrooms. Other shelves held bottles and jars of varying sizes. All were filled to the brim with a variety of wild berry jams and catsups which we had sealed with a layer of protective paraffin wax. Huge turnips hung by raveling rope from their yellow stalks; cabbages hung in a similar fashion by their dirt clinging roots. A record potato crop was concealed in several large wooden storage bins lining the back wall. In addition, we'd transported some of the things in our cabin to the chalet including what seemed to be our never ending supply of long, olive drab luncheon meat cans containing corned beef and spam. Dad planned to go moose hunting as soon as the weather kept cold enough to store fresh meat. I could easily picture the large quarters hanging from the meat rack he'd already made between two large trees only a slight way from the cabin door. We'd have plenty of good food and firewood to see us through the coming winter. And now that the surrounding mountains had received their first blanket of snow, I knew it wouldn't be long before the first few white flakes settled in our little valley.

During our first winter, I'd been anxious to see snow. We'd come from San Francisco, and I'd never seen a real snowfall. I remembered that Panda was born in our little cabin on September 23rd – the night of our first snowfall. She'd be a year old in another month. That meant it had been more than a year since we'd arrived at Gold Creek. At first I missed television and ice cream. But Dad said there were more important things than city conveniences, like being together and growing together as a family. So John and I had kept busy exploring our new home until that life we'd left in the city seemed like it had happened a million years ago.

CHAPTER 2
The Trappers

"Mush." John held a willow switch in his hand.

Panda, hitched single file behind Princess, lunged forward and grabbed onto her mother's wagging tail. Princess swerved, nipped her pup on the ear, and from then on our dog team went out of control.

"I told you not to hitch up Panda." I jumped from the little homemade sled we crowded together on and grabbed the rope that attached the dogs to the sled. Princess managed to get those same traces wrapped around her hocks. Panda, tongue hanging out, turned circles around John who had jumped from the sled with me. She tangled his legs in the rope that attached her harness. He lost his balance and fell backwards into the snow.

"Stupid dog." John grabbed a snap that fastened Panda to the sled. It crept forward, running halfway over my brother's body before he disengaged the pup from the sled. "Just turn them loose." He threw the sled to one side.

Freed now, Panda teased Princess who jerked at her traces, pulling me along with her. Snow funneled its way up past my mittens and into the cuffs of my coat as well as down the front. With John's help, we let her go and watched our runaway team continue their playful romp up the water trail and towards home. I pulled off my mittens and shook the snow from my sleeves.

"I'll bet Whitey doesn't have to put up with that."

"Yeah. But he's had more experience too." John brushed off his jeans. "Let's go."

Back in the cabin, Mom and Dad sat at the table going over homemade plans for a new house. Mom wanted it built on the higher part of the ridge, overlooking the first slough and the field. At Dad's request Mr. Ihly, our neighbor, had dug out a large area on the ridge top the previous fall after clearing our land. It was supposed to be the basement of our new house, but right then it was just a big ugly boulder strewn pit that had filled up with snow.

Dad rolled up the plans. "We probably can't build next year because we'll have to buy a Cat and clear ten more acres of land before we can apply for the patent to the homestead. But the year after that, watch out."

Mom helped clear the table.

"Will I have my own bedroom?" I took off my coat.

"You and everybody else." Mom gathered a few pencils together. "And the ceilings will be tall. There will be real glass windows all over with plenty of light coming in all winter long. We're even going to have an indoor bathroom."

"Will the house be as big as Botner's place?"

"Bigger, and two stories high with a pitched roof so we won't have to shovel snow off like Botner had to with his roof."

I couldn't imagine building a house bigger and better than Botner's. John and I went up there often just to look in the windows at the big kitchen, bedrooms and living room. There were sheds full of farm equipment too. Even a sawmill that Botner had made his own lumber with still rested in the cottonwood trees along the banks of Gold Creek, where he'd left it.

Sandra and Gay came inside now, giggling.

"How are we going to get the money to build it?" I asked.

"We can use the silver dollars," John suggested.

The Karo syrup can of silver dollars that Mom had made as tips when she worked as a waitress before we had left San Francisco were still safely stored under my parents' bed. When I'd gotten bored during the past winter, I sometimes asked Mom if I could count and date them. She'd always said yes, and I always forgot to write down how many we had. But I knew it was a whole bunch.

Mom wiped the table with a dish rag. "We'll be able to build when the time comes."

"We just took a walk along the ridge and saw all kinds of tracks down by the mouth of the first slough." Gay unwrapped her scarf.

"Probably mink." Dad put a rubber band around the plans. "They'll be following the Susitna River looking for open spots in the ice to fish from."

"Let's go look." John jumped up, closing his textbook.

"Not until you finish your reading," Mom warned.

"I am finished." John threw his body back into the chair.

Mom eyed him a few seconds. "Okay, you can go. But be back in time to meet the south bound passenger train. The Ihlys are leaving for Anchorage today and I think everyone should be at the section house to see them off."

"We will be." John sprang up again, grabbing his boots out from under the stove. He dressed quickly, then headed for the chalet to pick up a few traps. I dashed off to the outhouse, grabbed a roll of toilet tissue and concealed it under my coat. We met at the top of the water trail where John stood with a gunny sack over his shoulder.

The dogs followed us with Panda grabbing a free ride on our snowshoes whenever she could get away with it and shortly after we reached the snow covered frozen mouth of the first slough. We shooed the dogs back up our freshly made trail so they wouldn't trample the tracks we looked at.

"They're mink tracks all right." John unslung the traps.

"How do you know?"

"I know from what Dad told me. I think we should make a set here." He stood in the center of a white mound which in the summertime would have been a sandbar.

In the summertime the first slough was a spring–fed trickle of water which started near the base of the ridge our where our cabin sat. It was barely more than a water hole at its source, but by the time it had negotiated the base of the ridge for about a half mile and met the Big Susitna River, it had developed into a body of water several hundred yards across.

"With what?" I looked at the barren white blanket of snow surrounding us.

John looked around. "We'll build a teepee out of alders and set a couple of traps inside."

"What are we going to use for bait?"

"This." John opened the gunny sack and pulled out a piece of salt salmon. He dropped the fish on the ground then unsheathed his knife and headed for a nearby alder thicket.

"You're going to get into trouble if Mom and Dad find out you're using good food for bait." I stared at the large specimen. "Maybe we could use just a little of it and put the rest back."

"Are you kidding? We're going to need that much to make the mink think it's worthwhile to come into the set." He threw an alder in my direction.

"Okay. But I hope we don't get caught."

"The only thing that's going to get caught are mink, and plenty of them. "John tossed another alder.

I picked up the two frozen limbs, sticking them into the snow. Soon we had a little branch hut with several small openings for any game to enter through.

"Give me the fish." John leaned down to look inside the little hut for a place to hang the bait.

"Just a minute." I grabbed the piece of salmon, rubbing it on the traps and down the chains.

"What are you doing?" John sat up. "Do you want the mink to smell out the traps?"

"Whitey says you have to cover up the metal smell."

"Just give me the fish will you?" He held out his hand.

I hurriedly completed my job. John reached inside the hut and hung the bait with a piece of rope to one of the sturdier alders.

"Okay. Help me set these traps and be careful not to catch yourself."

"I know how to set traps." I grabbed one. I'd been practicing setting traps in the woodshed all summer.

By the time I had my trap set, John already had his in position inside the teepee. I placed mine at the opposite entrance, covered the chain and pole with snow, then pulled the roll of toilet tissue from my pocket.

"Can't you wait until we get home?" John moaned.

"This is for the traps." I unrolled several sheets, carefully placing the paper over the exposed jaws and spring. "Whitey says you have to cover your traps with paper and snow. Otherwise the animals will see them and walk around them."

John cocked his head slightly, watching me finish the operation "Give me some of that." He extended his hand again.

The dogs had become bored with trapping long ago and left for home. We followed, but before I went back into the cabin I ran to the outhouse, replacing the borrowed roll of tissue. By the time I got back, everyone else waited for me and we snowshoed the trail to the section house together.

"I sure wish you weren't going, Madge." Mom hugged Mrs. Ihly.

"We'll be back early in the spring. It just gets too cold up here for me all winter long. Make sure some of you come in to visit."

I started packing the loose snow under my big white insulated boots. They were army surplus boots and were called 'bunny boots' for no reason anybody knew. I'd decided they got their name because were so big they looked like I had the back feet of a rabbit. I continued to muse about my feet and waited for the train from Fairbanks to round the north bend. I'd only been into Anchorage once. That had been the previous March during the Fur Rendezvous. All the dog mushers and trappers came into town then to race their dogs and sell their winter's catch. I hoped we'd catch enough fur to do that.

The train thundered over the Big Susitna River Bridge, just around the bend in front of us. Mr. Ihly stepped into the middle of the tracks with his flashlight to flag it down. Seconds later, we waved to the couple through the glass windows of the coach cars.

"Can we really go visit?" I shouted to Mom. The moving cars created a face numbing breeze as they picked up speed.

"Maybe. It depends on whether or not we need things from town." She looked after the red lantern light of the caboose.

"When I go to town I'm going to have a real honest–to–goodness hamburger." John, who had already taken the lead home, talked over his shoulder. "With lettuce, onions, tomatoes, and a great big order of greasy french fries."

"Not me." Gay shook her head. "I'd like to watch TV."

"Yeah, with a great big banana split smothered in whipped cream, hot fudge and a big red cherry on top," I added.

Sandra didn't say anything. She just gave Mom a long blank stare then lagged behind the rest of us on the way home.

We all settled for a moose steak dinner and the Sunday afternoon radio shows instead. I munched excitedly on some homemade fudge through the Green Hornet, then went to bed while Mom and Dad stayed up to listen to both Northwind and Mukluk Telegraph. They were two short message programs on different Anchorage radio stations that sent personal news items to people in the bush.

The messages usually had something to do with departures and arrivals of people to and from the 'boondocks'. Sometimes we'd hear

Nick Botner get a message. After he had sold his homestead at Gold Creek, he started a hunting and fishing lodge at Stephan Lake, 30 miles east of Gold Creek. The only way you could get to Stephan Lake was by bush plane. We hadn't received any messages yet but Mrs. Ihly said she'd send us one when they were ready to come back to Gold Creek next spring. I fell asleep before the program ended.

"C'mon. Let's go." John shook me awake.

I opened my eyes and saw only his head and shoulders as he pulled the covers off my top bunk. "We've got to check that mink set."

I hopped out of bed. Mom and Dad were still sleeping in their bed only a half–dozen feet away. And I knew Gay and Sandra were in the loft because the folding ladder was down. I got dressed and cinched my big bunny boots tight.

CHAPTER 3
Whitey's Fault

In the next few weeks when we took salt fish from the barrel we substituted more rocks from the spring to keep the brine level up so Mom and Dad wouldn't get suspicious. Time after time our marauding mink slipped past our traps and stole the bait. We finally solved that problem by using wire instead of rope to hang the fish. But other challenges replaced it.

One time the weight of a heavy snowfall set off our traps long before our intended quarry arrived on the scene. Another time we'd approached the set with high hopes only to realize that we had let the set look so natural, the mink ran right by without even noticing the hut and its offering.

That particular morning, after having several days of thawing weather followed by a drop in temperature so drastic that even our water hole in the spring froze over, I again followed behind John to check the trapline. I tried not to step on another stolen piece of salt fish. John had tied it by a length of rope to the back end of his snowshoe. Since the time the mink missed the set completely, we'd decided we needed a smelly trail to lead him in. Sure enough, we now picked up fresh mink tracks crossing back and forth over our snowshoe trail. They were headed right to the hut.

"Do you want to look?" John stopped in front of the set.

I already saw tracks leaving the set and shook my head.

"Well, let's see why we missed him this time." John twisted his feet out of the siwash binding and knelt down by the entrance.

"Looks like he did a jig right on top of the traps." My brother broke a stick off the hut and carefully prodded one of the trap pans. "They're frozen open."

The other traps suffered from the same problem, and while John busied himself snapping and resetting the traps, I unrolled several lengths of new toilet tissue.

"That stuff isn't working. He shook his head when I handed him a length. "We're just as well off covering them with snow."

I hesitated, still holding onto the tissue. John finally took it, and job finished, we headed home.

Back at the cabin, Mom was using the table for rolling a pie crust, so when we came inside, I picked up my school books and studied on my bunk. Sandra was really concentrating on her lessons. Dad said she and Mom had settled into a cold war, which, to me, was better than when they sniped at each other. Mom seemed to turn all her energy to prodding John to do his lessons and she often caught Gay, books open in front of her, daydreaming or doodling a freehand sketch. Gay wasn't even in the cabin right then. On our way in, I'd seen her petting and talking to the dogs. When she entered a bit later, I looked up from my books.

"Did you notice that big red splotch on Panda's chest?" She asked. "It looks like she's losing her fur. Princess has something like it too, on her tummy."

"Let's go see." I put my text down and we went outside without our coats.

"What do you think it is?" I watched as Gay held Panda's neck back to expose a red area under the fur on her chest. Yellow pustules stuck out where Gay had pulled some loose hair free.

"I don't know. But it sure stinks. And look at her pale gums." Gay slipped her hands up to Panda's muzzle. The dog struggled very little.

"She hasn't eaten her dinner the past few days either." John joined us.

We stood back, looking at Panda. Her tail hung limp between her legs and her eyes appeared sunken.

"Isn't there something we can do for her?" Gay petted the silky head.

"I don't know. What about Princess?" I started walking over to our Samoyed. She greeted us enthusiastically.

I discovered only a slight tender redness on Princess' tummy. She seemed barely affected by the soreness. In the meantime, Panda had rolled up in a little furry ball and was lying next to the spruce tree that fastened her chain.

"She really looks miserable," John said as the three of us went back to the cabin.

"I don't know what to do about it." Mom shook her head when we told her.

"We could take them into town for a veterinarian to look at," Gay suggested.

"No. We couldn't afford the trip. We've got to save every penny for the new Cat."

"Well there's just got to be something we can do." Tears filled Gay's eyes. "Panda's really suffering."

"When Dad comes back from hunting we'll have him take a look at her."

"I think it's cruel to let her suffer that way." Sandra looked up from a textbook. "Doug would never let a thing like that happen to his dogs."

Mom glared at her and she finally looked back down. Then I watched Mom pull a length of wax paper from a roll she kept stored near the sink, place the piece on the table surface and begin to roll out another crust.

"I don't know why I didn't think of it before." I hurried along beside John that same afternoon on our way to check the mink set with the appropriated roll of paper under my coat. "Wax paper is the answer. It won't soak up moisture like toilet tissue and then the traps won't freeze."

"I hope you're right." John looked doubtful.

There were no new tracks around the set. We weren't surprised to find the traps frozen open again. Knocking each free of ice, we reset and covered them with individual squares of paper. Then we sprinkled a fine layer of snow over the floor of the set and traps.

"We've got him this time for sure." John talked more on the way home. When we got there, Dad was standing with the rest of the family next to Panda. He still had his rifle in his hand.

"What is it?" I asked Dad, who patted Panda lightly on her head then knelt down to examine the growing sore patch on her chest as well as her gums.

"I don't know. Her gums look yellow, like she's been poisoned, but that could be a side effect of the other problem." Dad kept her from nuzzling his ear. He stood up. "I'm afraid I'm going to have to take Panda away."

"You mean take her to a vet?"

"No. I doubt a vet could help her now, even if we could take her. Panda's going to have to be shot."

"You can't do that," I pleaded.

"Little Darlin's suffering. I can't stand to see her go on like this day after day until she dies. When's the last time she ate?"

None of us answered.

"I'm afraid I have no other choice." Dad slipped the dog's collar off.

"Give her until tomorrow, at least." Gay followed behind as he encouraged Panda to follow him down the water trail and into the field. "Maybe she'll be better."

"No, honey. She won't be better. It's got to be this way. Now I want everybody to go back into the cabin."

Mom herded us together as Dad and Panda disappeared down the water trail. Inside, we turned on the radio and listened to Christmas carols until Dad returned.

"She didn't even know what hit her." Dad sat down.

Mom placed a cup of hot coffee in front of him. He stared at the steam rising lazily from the surface.

"What about Princess?" Gay sobbed. "Are we going to shoot her too?"

"Not if we can find out how to stop that infection from spreading. I'll write Whitey. He might know what to do." Dad picked up the cup.

Whitey's trapping cabin was about twelve miles from the tracks. So even when Dad put the letter on the next day's train, I knew the chances of Whitey coming all the way in from his cabin to collect his mail at the Chulitna section house that same day weren't too good. By the following Sunday, we still hadn't heard from him and Princess was getting sicker. To make our problems worse, we'd missed the mink several more times. It seemed the animal knew just where the traps were and avoided them. When we got to the mouth of the slough that afternoon, we tore the hut apart and made it slightly larger but with tighter walls. Then we set every trap we had in the shed. There was no way the mink could tunnel up under the snow to the inside of the hut or sniff curiously around the outside walls without setting something off.

"That should do it." John stood back.

We heard the south bound passenger train then and hurried home. When I saw Gay standing out by Princess crying, I knew we'd heard from the sourdough.

"Whitey says he thinks the dogs have mange." She looked up as we approached. "He said that if the infections reached the point where the dogs were off their food and had yellow gums that all we could do was put them out of their misery."

I glanced at Princess who'd lost a lot of weight in the past few days and like Panda lacked her usual energy. "But how could she get mange?" I double checked her gums, fighting the tears.

"From the harnesses. Whitey told Dad he forgot to mention that we should have boiled them first. He lost two of his own dogs the same way last year."

"Oh, no." I knelt, keeping Princess from licking my face.

The cabin door opened and I turned. Dad, a length of rope and rifle in his hand, came towards us.

"Maybe she'll get better," I pleaded as he slipped the rope around her neck. "She's not as bad as Panda was."

"You don't want her to suffer as long as Panda did, do you?" Mom stood by watching.

"No. But there's a chance she might be okay."

"No, there isn't. Not up here," Dad said firmly.

John stood next to me now, his own eyes watering.

We refused to go inside this time. Instead we stood on the ridgeside and watched Dad lead Princess down to the river. I closed my eyes when the shot came.

"I hate Whitey Rudder." I squeezed my eyes so tightly they ached. "I hate him."

"Whitey didn't mean to hurt us or the dogs." Gay stood by me.

"I'll never forgive him for it." I clenched my fists and opened my eyes to see Dad coming back from far across the field.

"Just how do you think he feels. He had to shoot her."

"I don't care how he feels. All I care about is how I feel."

Gay turned away from the ridge. I waited a few minutes then followed.

The next morning John shook me awake. With the cabin still quiet we sneaked outside, slipped into our snowshoes and started off for the mouth of the first slough. The foot of fresh snow stretched in an unmarred layer of white all around. At the set, we twisted out of our shoes, using them for shovels. I found a trap chain and pulled.

"Hey, I think we got something." I dug with both hands.

"Be careful about going in there like that." John grabbed another chain, pulling.

"No. I mean it. We really got something!"

John tugged on his chain, then joined me on his hand and knees. "I've got him! I've got him!" John yelled, pulling.

"No. I do." I yanked at my chain.

"It's a mink!" John's eyes widened as the dead, dark–furred animal flung into his lap after a jerk on one of the trap chains.

"Are you sure?"

"Of course I'm sure. Dad told me all about them." My brother freed the limp weasel–like body from the traps. "Let's go show him."

I slipped into my shoes, running behind my brother as he talked about how much bigger our trapline would be next year now that we knew how to do it. I wanted to expand our trapline too. But couldn't help feeling that, thanks to Whitey Rudder, we'd have to do it without a dog team.

CHAPTER 4
If You Blink

Spring came early in 1962. With my seventh grade schoolwork behind me already, I anxiously watched it arrive. John, with help and Mom's encouragement, had also finished the eighth grade by the time our new Cat was taken off a flat car at the Gold Creek siding. But Gay, still drawing pictures on her notebook paper, had not yet completed the ninth grade. On the day Dad drove our shiny piece of machinery into the field and scraped off the first bladeful of overburden, my older sister had been restricted to the cabin with Sandra.

The remaining four in our family took to the field daily, up before the morning dew burned off. After a big breakfast and with a supply of cold drinks in hand, we tackled the job. We'd only been working in the field for several weeks now, but my body had lost the original soreness that wakened me during the night after those first few days of bone-wearying labor. Our little Cat didn't have the power of Mr. Ihly's D4 and often balked at heavy passes Dad made into the overburden. But the little piece of machinery continued to gnaw away steadily at the native growth, just as I'd forced myself to return to the field each day with the others.

Heaving a large rock into a small gully, I turned, wiping my forehead with the back of a dirty sleeve. A late June sun beat on us unmercifully, but I preferred hot days like this one to clouds or rain. Heat meant fewer mosquitoes were out to bother us as we ripped back the layer of cool muskeg, destroying their hiding and breeding places. Muskeg was a peculiar sort of vegetation. It covered the earth in a mat which peeled back like a carpet when the Cat blade was applied. Last summer I'd started building a little fort out of squares of muskeg I'd cut free from the forest floor. But by the time the walls of my fort reached only knee high I'd tired of the project.

The smell of fresh earth reached me and I stood a few minutes watching Dad operate the Cat far across the field. Mom and John worked near me, picking up the roots and rocks exposed during the clearing operation. When Dad shut the Cat engine down, they too looked up.

"Don't tell me he slipped another track." Mom stood, hands on her hips.

John shaded his eyes. "Sure looks like it."

"Go get the bars then. It looks like the rest of the afternoon is going to be spent getting that thing back together again."

Mom started towards the Cat with an uneven stride over the freshly torn dirt. She'd tucked her jean bottoms into the top of combat boots to keep insects from crawling up her legs. The tail of a torn long sleeved shirt had pulled out from a similar tucking around her waist and hung flapping around her thighs. The sleeves, rolled up to elbow length, exposed darkly tanned forearms. On her head, a floppy wide brimmed rain hat, used today to protect her face from the sun, didn't quite manage to cover some of her hair and it jutted out along the hat's edges. I watched the walking scarecrow hop from one hummock to another, each lunge taking her a little farther away.

"We might as well get to it." John turned.

I followed him to the edge of the spring, picked up a long steel pry bar and placed it over my shoulder. John did likewise. Resisting the temptation to stop for a drink, we made our way across the field to the silent Cat. Slipping a track on the Cat had become common enough to annoy all of us. Sometimes Dad would push a load and turn too abruptly on the rough surface, forcing the track on one side to jump the rim on either the front or rear wheel. If the track hadn't slipped too badly, just a small stick placed between the portion of the track which had slipped would bring it back in line. If, however, it had slipped all the way off the front or rear wheel, Dad needed to loosen the track and we had to pry the heavy linked plates back into place with the bars.

When we reached the Cat, both Mom and Dad sat on its slipped appendage, waiting.

"The front is off to the outside, the back to the inside." Dad motioned. "I think we're going to be working on this one the rest of the afternoon."

He stood up, took the large crescent wrench John had also brought along, then sat facing the track. I watched him work for awhile, then looked out over the area we'd cleared. We needed to clear and plant a total of twenty acres in order to meet federal government homesteading regulations. Mom said it seemed silly to clear, till and plant land way out in the middle of nowhere. But that's what was required in order to get the patent on our land, so that was what we were doing.

We were going to plant timothy, rye and clover for our crop. It was easy to grow and would reseed itself.

Later that afternoon as Dad retightened the track nuts from another incident Mom left for the cabin to help Sandra and Gay prepare dinner.

"I can handle it from here." Dad cinched the track down and looked up at John. "You and Melody go get cleaned up. I'll see you back at the cabin."

Hot and tired, we nonetheless raced over the hummocks to the second slough. Here at the mouth the channel of spring-fed water was deep and wide because a beaver had built a dam and dug out the silty bottom. I stripped off my clothes and dove into the crystal clear water. The second slough was anything but warm. However, compared to the first slough, which was spring fed and ice cold, we at least found it tolerable. That was because the second slough got its water from river overflow which was then partially trapped by the beaver dam to become somewhat sun-warmed. What I liked about the slough best though was its location. It was far across the field from the cabin. Large towering cottonwood trees on our very own island, around which the slough wrapped itself, assured privacy.

A cannon-like sound startled me as the beaver pounded out his intruder alarm to the rest of the forest with a sharp blow of his flat, scaly tail. I ignored several more warnings and he finally disappeared below the surface.

By the time I'd finished bathing, John already stood on the bank toweling himself down. His face, neck and forearms were deeply tanned but the rest of his body remained pale. Had we been able to sun bathe like both Gay and Sandra, we too could have developed an even body tan. But field work required full clothing for protection.

"C'mon. We'll be late for supper if you don't hurry." John rubbed down his hair with a dingy white towel.

I swam to the mouth of the slough and stood on a sandbar for a few minutes while the sun worked at returning warmth to my numb body. In front of me a swift channel of the Susitna River met the slough. I watched as my sinking toes released silt into the clear slough water before the passing current sucked it out.

"Are you coming?" John, pants and boots on, carried the rest of his clothes.

I turned and splashed through the shallows, slipped into my pants and gathered up the rest of my clothes. John had already replaced the soap, shampoo and towel in a nearby willow patch.

"I don't know how you stand to run around in your bare feet that way." John screwed up his face. "Doesn't that hurt?"

"No." I tied my boot laces together and flung them over a shoulder.

"I'll bet if you scraped all that callous off the bottom of your feet you wouldn't be as tall as I am anymore." John scurried up the bank and I followed.

Bare feet or not, I kept pace with my older brother as we ran through the field. John stopped at the spring, scooping up a dipperful of the alder-shaded water while I wiggled my field dirty feet in the cold stream just down from him. Then back at the cabin and copying John, I swung a leg over the back of my chair and plopped down in front of the dinner table with the rest of the family.

"Dad and I thought that since we quit a little early today we'd go visit the Ihlys' across the creek." Mom had changed into a more flattering and clean set of work clothes. "We might be back late so don't any of you bother to wait up."

The Ihlys had moved to their homestead across Gold Creek when they came back that spring. Mr. Ihly built a wooden bridge across the creek so his jeep could get across during high water. Their homestead house was the exact replica of the one they had near Botner's place, except it was painted green instead of red. Mom began clearing dishes before I'd finished my grouse stew. Then both of my parents applied liberal amounts of mosquito dope and left.

I finished my dinner, deposited the plate in the sink and lay down on the bunk while Sandra started up another endless conversation with Gay about Doug.

"He's bought a cabin up at Chulitna where he's living right now. It's on a hill above a beautiful lake and the view of Mt. McKinley is breathtaking."

"Is he going to live up there?" Gay asked.

"Just for this summer so we can be close, even though Mom and Dad won't let us see each other. When winter comes, Doug is going into town to get a job. Then when I come into town this December, we'll be married."

"So you'll live in Anchorage?"

"Of course. Doug promised me we won't live in the bush. He'd never stick me in a God-forsaken place like this."

"It wouldn't be so God-forsaken if you didn't make it that way," I said.

Sandra laughed. "Well, Meddy, if you weren't so busy being Mommy and Daddy's little pet you'd be able to see how ridiculous this whole thing is. If I could leave, no one would have to be suffering."

I pulled the pillow over my head. I hated it when she called me Meddy. She was the only one in the family who did. Ever since Doug started calling her Sandy she insisted on that name for herself. He even got her a belt with the name SANDY on it. But I still called her Sandra. Sometimes Gay called me Mudz, which was kind of cute. But I didn't think Meddy was cute at all.

Despite Sandra's constant chatter, I finally fell asleep. Then some time later, silence awakened me. The sky outside our back cabin window was either fading out from the dark blue of late afternoon or getting ready to turn into a darker blue, signaling a new day. I couldn't readily tell which. Mom and Dad were not in their bed and the rest of the family slept. I sat up and searched out the ticking clock on the night stand near the far bed, focusing in on it.

Six o'clock. But was it six o'clock in the morning or evening? The sun, high in the sky, gave me no clue. I heard birds singing, but they sang all night during the summer, so that didn't help either. This kind of day-night limbo in the summertime confused me with light, just as wintertime sometimes confused me with dark. Being so close to the Arctic Circle gave us constant daylight in June, but we had to pay the price in the winter when in December there was almost constant darkness. I hopped out of my bunk and opened the cabin door.

It was a new day. We'd been losing daylight for a week or so. Soon the sun would rise a little farther down the mountainous horizon, and finally, in December, we'd lose it entirely. Then in February, if a person wanted to keep a close lookout for the first day of its return, a glimmer of the heatless yellow disc could be caught in the dip between the mountains where Gold Creek cut through the crests. As Mrs. Ihly had so aptly described, "If you blink, you'll miss it."

Voices carried on the early morning air alerted me. I went around the side of the cabin where Mom's laughter floated down from the section house trail. I ran to meet them. Dad grinned broadly.

"Had a pretty good time, huh?" I grinned back.

"Oh, my sides just ache. We laughed so much I can hardly stand to breathe."

"Are we going to work in the field today?"

"Nope. Mom and I are declaring a holiday. You kids can go fishing if you want."

We did. But, the next morning when I awakened to the sound of pouring rain on our tarpapered roof, I knew we'd taken the wrong day off.

The heavy rainfall made field work difficult and we worked in silence. By mid–morning the ground got too muddy for Dad to clear any more land for fear he'd get stuck or slip a track. Instead, he joined us while we hauled debris into the windrows along the edge of the field. We'd nearly completed clearing our acreage. Dad told us that Nick Ihly had offered to lend us his plow to cultivate our land if we would help saw up some large trees that needed hauling out of his field. As rain soaked through the back of my shirt that afternoon, I worked and tried to calculate how much longer we'd be doing field jobs that year. At the end of it, Dad promised us a caribou hunt on the mountain.

I heard the northbound passenger train stop at the section house. Then sometime later we all raised our heads to a distant 'hallo'. A man and young boy came towards us, collars turned up against the rain. I didn't recognize them, but as the man came closer a friendly smile crossed his face. He extended a hand to Dad, pumping it energetically.

"I'm Bill Maddock," he said. "And you must be Leon and Alice Erickson."

I watched the young boy with him, gauging us to be about the same age. He stood with his shoulders scrunched against the rain as if feeling every drop that hit. When he looked over at me through squinting eyes, I picked up a huge root remnant, tossed it onto a pile, then stood letting the rain run through my long straight hair and down my face.

"The girls at the cabin told me I'd find you down here," the man continued.

"What can we do for you?" Dad wiped droplets from his nose with the back of his sleeve.

"I just bought the Botner place."

"Well. Welcome aboard." Dad grinned.

But the man shook his head. "Not so fast," he laughed. "My family lives in Anchorage. I'm a doctor there. We just bought the place for an investment and I was wondering if I could impose upon you people to look after the place for us. Of course, we'd be glad to pay you for any time you spend." The man paused.

"It won't be necessary to pay us. We'd be glad to watch the place for you. The kids go by it several times a month anyway, fishing or hunting." Dad gestured towards John and me.

"Well then, I want you to feel free to use whatever equipment he has stored up there. It looks to me like you're going to be doing a lot of cultivating and planting this year and could use some of the stuff. Whatever you can make use of is yours. In fact, I'd feel better if it were down here at your place all the time instead of up there in those open sheds."

"That's very generous of you," Mom said.

"Nonsense. The equipment is there. You might as well put it to use." He shook Dad's hand again. "I must say you folks have the stuff the backbone of this state is made of, living out here like this. Takes guts, sheer guts." He stopped pumping Dad's hand and glanced over at John, then at the boy with him. "Loosen up a little, son. The rain isn't going to melt you."

We watched them retreat across the field. The man stepped lively, the boy barely keeping up.

"Well, what do you know about that! We've got all of Botner's farm equipment." Dad kept his eyes on the departing figures.

"Yeah." John came closer. "There's a disc, harrow, seeder, all types of planters. You name it, Botner had it."

"I guess we'd better get back to work and finish this job off." Dad sent a large rock sailing off the edge of the field. "With all that equipment we'll have this field in better shape than any other one in Gold Creek, and in record time."

I liked that thought. The trip up the mountain for a caribou wasn't far from my grasp. John had gotten his first caribou the previous year when he was twelve. I was anxious to match his record.

CHAPTER 5
Something's Rotten

    I sat facing backwards on top of the plow, legs dragging. My bare heels bumped over clods of dirt as the heavy discs cut into virgin ground. The added weight of my small body helped the discs sink deeper into the soil, exposing a rich topsoil we'd soon be planting. Not far behind, my brother kept pace with the Cat and plow. He bent over occasionally to toss a stone or piece of wood off the end of the field. I glanced past him and at the thousands of rows of freshly-tilled dirt to focus on the deep V cut between Nevermore and Disappointment mountains and licked my dust covered lips. Although I couldn't see it, I knew that was where Gold Creek's cool refreshing spray tumbled. My thoughts turned to our fall caribou hunt and I studied the mountains. Nevermore was difficult to climb, but the game was plentiful on top. Disappointment was just the opposite. There was a better view of Gold Creek valley from Disappointment, but there was always the possibility we'd get skunked on a hunt.

    "Hey. How about letting me ride and you pick up junk for awhile?" John yelled over the noise of the straining Cat.

    Reluctantly, I relinquished my metal throne to assume John's position behind the heavy plow. September had again found our little valley, and we raced against winter to get all our field work done. We'd already completely cultivated and planted half of the acreage and had nearly finished the ten acres cleared that summer. Now, still trodding behind the plow, I made another of my perpetual calculations of the work to be done. I had hoped that within a week's time I would stand on the ridge and look down at 20 acres of level, tilled, planted ground. The following spring we would witness the previous fall's labor grow into lush waves of timothy grass.

    Just because we were near finishing our job in the field though, didn't mean John, Dad or I could sit back, relax and watch winter come. We still needed to harvest our garden crop, cut wood for the winter and, when Dad finally decided the right time had come, climb the mountain for a caribou. All this needed to be done before our school books arrived.

Back at the cabin, Gay still struggled with the ninth grade. Sandra, on the other hand, progressed rapidly in her studies. She said that when she left in December on her eighteenth birthday, a day she'd termed her 'Independence Day', she would have only a half year of high school to finish. She intended to pick that up at night school in Anchorage. My oldest sister had continued to look forward to that train trip out of Gold Creek, especially since early August, when Mom had left for town at the same time the Ihlys had left for the winter. Several days later Mom had sent a Mukluk Telegraph saying she'd gotten a job. Dad said she had gone into town to work for money in order to make the Cat payments. But I figured she wanted to get away from Sandra.

Occasionally Mom would send some beef up with the other groceries we had ordered. But after a five hour train ride in the hot baggage car, even a tightly wrapped frozen delicacy starting on its trip in the morning ended up brown and dripping by the time the train pulled into Gold Creek. I'd developed a taste for wild game anyway and as a result, John and I still hunted grouse, squirrel, even porcupine, with Ren, our little Shetland sheep dog. But hunting, like fishing, meant taking time out from work so we'd not been able to hunt for many fresh meat meals. Long ago we had used up all the canned meat from the previous year's hunt. So we once again found ourselves back down to those huge drab green containers of corned beef, spam and that summer's restocked supply of canned salmon.

Sometimes Gay would make her famous 'meatless stew'. This was a concoction of all the garden fresh root crops mixed with canned creamed corn. The creamed corn was something we'd bought and had frozen when the stove fire in the chalet had gone out by accident one time the previous winter. By itself the corn looked awful, but mixed with the other vegetables it wasn't half bad.

Dad pulled the Cat up short now and I nearly ran into the back of the plow. "Let's call it quits for today," he shouted, leaning over to push the engine kill button. "We'll get an early start tomorrow."

Neither John nor I complained. We stopped with Dad to pick some garden vegetables, washed them off in the spring and headed up the water trail.

Inside the cabin, Sandra arranged a dozen red roses in a vase.

Gay stood by with a scissors, helping her trim the stems to different lengths.

"Look what Doug sent Sandra from Anchorage." Gay put a snipped stalk in a long empty box that lay open on the table. "Aren't they just beautiful?"

"They're very nice." Dad sat down, glancing around while John and I put the dripping vegetables on the drainboard. "What's for dinner?"

"Oh, I don't know." Sandra fussed with the flowers.

"You mean you've been up here all day and haven't even started dinner?" Dad stood up, going over to the stove. He lifted a lid. "What's going on here anyway? Are you too busy to keep a fire going?" He hefted the coffee pot. "There's no coffee either." Dad slammed the container down and I jumped.

"Now listen, you two. Mom isn't here to do all this work anymore and as far as I'm concerned your vacation is over. When we come up from the field I want to see the cabin clean, a fire going, fresh coffee and a dinner on the table. Is that clear?"

Gay scurried to put all the flower scraps in the box.

"Just look at the mess this cabin is in." He continued. "There isn't an hour's worth of work a day in here to keep it clean. I'm certain that between your girl talk and giggling sessions you can find at least that much time. We're working hard out there all day. We don't need to come into this pig sty and be forced to cook our own meals, too."

Gay dumped the box next to the stove for burning. "It's no fun being stuck in this hot cabin all day doing schoolwork either, you know. Or trying to figure out what to make for dinner all the time. We're getting just as tired of cooking the same stuff day after day as you are eating it."

"Did any of us complain to you about the food? I don't recall that." Dad looked innocently at John and me.

"It's obvious from the faces John and Melody make and the way they play with their food that they don't like what we make." Sandra put the vase out of the way on a back dresser.

"If you hadn't made Mom leave, you wouldn't have to do it all by yourself," I blurted.

Dad ignored our comments. He looked at his pocket watch. "We're going back down in the field to dig potatoes, and when we come back I want to see this cabin clean, the table set, and dinner ready to eat. Do you think you can handle that?"

"Of course we can handle that." Sandra turned. "But I don't want to hear any complaints about what we're having for dinner."

"Just cook." Dad left and we followed.

A hour later Gay came down to the field to tell us supper was ready. We went up to the cabin, washed, and sat down at the table. I thought Gay and Sandra had done just about everything with corned beef that was possible. We'd eaten corned beef hash, chipped corned beef on toast, corned beef and eggs, and corned beef sandwiches. But that night as Sandra ladled out a concoction of creamed corned beef over mashed potatoes I couldn't help asking the question.

"What is that?"

"If you have to ask, you're not hungry," Dad thanked Sandra for the full plate of food he accepted.

I took my plate without further comment, then picked up a forkful and watched the pasty mixture drip through the tines. John was in a similar pose but with both sisters watching we quietly cleaned our plates.

"I can't take much more of that junk," John said from the side of the outhouse right after dinner.

"Maybe we could get Dad to go on a caribou hunt now instead of later."

"Naw. He won't go hunting until all the field work is done. He promised Mom."

"Well that can't be more than a week away. I think we should ask him anyway."

"No. Let's wait until the work is done and all the garden is taken care of. Then he won't be able to refuse."

We formed a pact and started out energetically to the field the next morning. When Dad wanted to quit discing early, we encouraged him to keep going and then afterwards finished digging and hauling the potatoes from the garden into the chalet. After dinner, something I tried not to taste, John joined me in the garden again where we pulled turnips, topped them and stored them in the chalet also. The following day Dad got caught up in our fervor and by the end of a long day I broadcast the last few acres of ground with a clover–timothy grass mixture while the two others stripped our garden of remaining produce. The morning of the third day we sat eating breakfast while Dad figured out the next thing that needed to be done. John brought up the hunt.

"We have to get wood in first. Then we'll talk about hunting." Dad finished his coffee.

"But getting enough wood in for winter could take weeks. A hunt is only going to take one day," John argued.

"First the wood, then hunting. The longer we wait, the cooler the weather, the longer we'll be able to keep the meat without having to can it." Dad deposited his cup in the sink.

All of us sat following Dad with our eyes as he left the cabin door.

"C'mon, let's go." John stood up. "We might as well get it over with."

My brother and I scraped our plates into the slop pail where I noticed Sandra had finally thrown the roses. They were way past the dead stage. Dad already had the Cat going with the stoneboat hooked up when we reached him. The chain saw and axes were already on it. We hopped aboard and stood bracing ourselves for the jerk we knew would come as Dad started the Cat moving.

"Hold on, I'm coming," Gay yelled and leaped onto the stoneboat just as it started to move.

He drove along a trail in the woods we'd made earlier that summer. Then only several hundred yards from the cabin, he turned the Cat and stoneboat around and killed the engine. He picked up the chain saw and pointed.

"John, you start notching that one to fall between those two spruce trees. Melody and Gay you take that one over there. Set it up to fall alongside the the road. I'm going to saw up that wind–fallen birch over there." Dad moved off the road with the saw.

We each walked to our designated jobs. Gay and I circled the birch tree Dad told us to notch. We peeled away some of the rough bark on its trunk, then looked up at the huge limbs, checking for widow–makers. The sharp ring of biting axes into sound wood filled the forest until the chain saw smothered our rhythm. After Dad cut our trees down, we carried the lengths onto the stoneboat. When it was loaded to capacity the three of us sat on top holding the lengths steady while Dad drove home. We hauled five more trees before quitting for the day. Upon entering the cabin that night, there was hot water in the teakettle for basin baths, a set table and a banana cream pie cooling outside on the porch.

"It looks like you put in a full day's work today, too," Dad said to Sandra as he sat down at the table.

Gay smiled while Sandra dished out corned beef hash and a fresh vegetable. I was too tired to do much more than pick at my food. But Dad had seconds before shoving his plate away from the edge of the table.

"Boy. I'm really stiff. I guess we're out of shape for hauling wood. Tomorrow we'll take it easy." Dad sat back in his chair and rubbed his arms.

"Does that mean we're going hunting?" John asked.

"No. I've got a special project lined up for us to do in the field. Then we'll get more wood."

"But we're finished in the field." I put my fork down.

"Not quite." Dad stood up. "And after that we've got to start chopping spruce trees for the new house to be built next year."

I picked up my utensil again, worrying a piece of fried potato, then shoved my plate away.

"Do you want some pie?" Gay asked.

"Naw. I'm not hungry." I stood up. "Maybe later."

"Hold my piece too," John said.

Sandra stood up now, busily clearing the table. "Well I don't know why we even bother to make a decent meal around here for all the appreciation we get."

"I'll have a piece of pie," I heard Dad say before the cabin door closed behind me.

I walked up the ridge, looking over the field we'd finally cleared, and tried to imagine what else could be done to it. The next morning we both followed Dad down to the garden plot where he handed me a shovel.

"I want you to dig a trench about a foot wide and two feet deep the length of the garden plot, starting right here." He pushed the shovel into the soft dirt with his booted heel.

"What for?" I moaned.

"A fertilizer trench. We're going to get those dead salmon out of the slough, throw them in here and bury them. John is going to help me gaff them. Unless of course you want to do that job while he digs the trench."

"No. No. That's okay. I'll dig." I grabbed up the shovel.

Dad, John following, picked up some gaff hooks and headed for the first slough. I dug in, heaving great mounds of dirt out of the trench. I'd seen what was left of those battered belly–up bodies after the salmon spawned and died. Some grew a fuzzy white fungus that I tried not to think about. Minutes later the smell of rotting fish preceded both Dad and John as both of them, gaff extended well behind, dragged several of the carcasses towards me. When they reached the trench I took several steps backwards. Dad flung his fish downwards. The rotting flesh ripped free from the metal gaff. John followed suit. Then, not saying anything, both went back for another load. Not looking at the trench's contents, I covered the corpses.

"What is that awful smell?" Gay came into the garden sometime later to salvage what remained of the lettuce crop.

"Dad and John are bringing rotten fish out of the slough."

"What an awful stench." Gay walked to the far end of the lettuce row. Then, giving me equally wide berth on the way back, she headed for the cabin.

By the time the next load of fish came in, I'd hardened my stomach somewhat to the smell. But none of us were hungry for lunch so we worked straight through until finishing the job late that afternoon. I figured we'd hauled and buried close to a hundred salmon and while washing up in the spring with the others, hoped it wouldn't be a job we repeated every year. The cool water splashing on my face revived me and I developed a ravenous appetite. Doubting Gay and Sandra had kept any lunch warm, I prepared myself for a long wait before dinner. But when we stepped into the little cabin, both Gay and Sandra sat at a set table. The doors and windows were open, making the little cabin bright and airy.

"Are you hungry?" Sandra stood up.

"Absolutely starved." John sat down at the table. "I don't care what you've made, just bring it on." He slapped a paper napkin open and positioned it on his lap.

"We kept the food warm." She brought a covered platter out of the oven.

Dad sat down, pulling the platter towards him. I scooped a gob of mashed potatoes out of another pot and passed it along to John while Dad raised the lid from the main dish. John didn't take the offered pot. Instead he stared at the uncovered plate. I followed his gaze to the pile of fried salmon patties.

Dad slammed the lid down, his face red. "Don't you know we've been dragging rotten salmon out of the slough all day?" He roared.

"How was I supposed to know?" Sandra looked amazed. "Melody and John are always complaining about the food so I thought it would be nice to have something different."

"Well I want something else in fifteen minutes." Dad stood up. "And get this smell out of here." Dad threw the platter of fish into the slop pail and headed outside with it.

"You've really done it now." John threw himself back into his chair while Sandra and Gay scurried to fix something else for dinner.

Sandra and Gay got another meal on the table in record time and we all waited for Dad's return.

Finally, the cabin door opened. Dad stepped inside carrying the garbage festooned bouquet of lifeless roses. Their browned curled leaves dripped the contents of the slop pail onto his grasping hand. He held them out towards Sandra.

"Are you really sure you're ready to throw these away so soon?" His eyes were serious but the corners of his mouth twitched.

From the disgusted look on Sandra's face, I knew Dad had gotten even.

CHAPTER 6
The Hunt

Muffled voices awakened me the next morning. I looked towards the front of the cabin to see Dad and John standing together, packboards on.

"What's happening?" I jumped down from my bunk.

"We're going caribou hunting," Dad said.

"Wait for me." I slipped into my jeans and pulled on a pair of boots. At Dad's insistence I gulped down a bowl of cereal while John waited impatiently.

By mid-morning I sat on a tundra knoll with my packboard on and 30-30 rifle nearby. We were halfway up Nevermore mountain. Steam rose off my dew soaked jeans as I looked into the valley far below us. The field was easy to pick out. But from the mountain, it was only the size of a ragged postage stamp.

"Who's going to shoot the caribou?" John popped some wild blueberries into his mouth.

"Whoever spots him first." Dad sat back. "But if you miss the first shot, he's fair game for the other hunters."

"Let's get on with it then." My brother reslung his rifle. "There's a caribou up on top with my name on him."

We clawed our way through patches of mountain alder and thorny devil's club to reach the top. An hour later I stood with them in a brisk tundra breeze. I leaned down, pulling a few white tufts of caribou moss out by the roots. The spongy plants looked like a miniature tangle of antlers and they crumbled easily between my thumb and index finger while I studied the rolling mountain tops in front of us. The carpet of plants clashed with vibrant yellows, reds and greens. Fall had come to the mountain. The fall we still waited for in the valley.

John and Dad began climbing the next rise and I started off behind them. Then I saw the unmistakable white dot of a caribou's chest. He'd evidently been browsing in a slight dip far off to our right and now meandered slowly back from the edge. Crouching down low, I ran up to the others.

"Over there," I whispered. "He's heading around the other side of that rise."

Dad looked in the direction I indicated. "I don't see anything."

"Me neither," John whispered.

"He's there all right. If we get over the other side of this hill and in front of him we can head him off."

Dad looked at me, then the area where I'd said the caribou was.

"Okay. Let's go." He paused to look at John. "And remember, Melody gets the first shot."

Quietly slipping a round into the chamber of my rifle, I crouched low and led the others up the hill. Judging where the caribou was when I first saw him and the speed he moved, I bee–lined it to the most likely spot on the horizon we'd cross paths. We were still on high ground and if my calculations were correct, the wind worked with us.

We came upon him so suddenly, I didn't have much time to prepare for the shot. He was a magnificent buck, but judging from the size of his rack, still young. The caribou had spotted us and stood still, sniffing the air. His antlers were framed against the clear blue sky and his chest was as white as a December snowball. Although I didn't dare move to look, I knew both Dad and John flanked me. John would be in a shooting position eager for his chance. Dad would be standing still, waiting for me to make the first move.

I raised my rifle slowly to my left shoulder. The caribou turned, eyeing me as I lined my V sight up with his chest. This was meat; rich red meat that fried up into juicy steaks we hadn't tasted for over a year. Meat that meant no more corned beef or salmon patties. I thought of meat and applied firm pressure to the trigger.

"Did you see that?" John slapped me on the back as we quickly covered the seventy–five yards between us and the fallen buck. "One shot and that caribou just turned right over on his back. All four legs went straight up in the air just like it was out of a comic strip." He laughed then added. "I thought you were never going to shoot."

"I was waiting for the right moment."

"It was a well–placed shot all right." Dad bent down, pulling his sideknife out. He turned the stilled head by its antlers. "Clean as a whistle."

I reached over and closed the eye.

"He didn't feel a thing," Dad added.

We helped Dad clean and quarter the caribou. Then each with a full load started back down the mountain. When we reached the tundra knoll we'd rested on that morning, we began dragging our packs. By the time we got to the bottom, the white caribou fur had turned the color of wild blueberries. The back straps cut into my shoulders as I again loaded up and followed the other packers down the trail. My feet seemed to have a mind of their own and, body set in automatic forward, my mind began to wander. I thought about getting home, retelling the hunt to Sandra and Gay, and writing Mom about my first caribou.

Dark closed around us before I heard Gold Creek's tumbling waters. A mile later my shoulders felt a sudden relief when I slipped out of the pack near the chalet. We strung the quarters from several log rafters inside the building then headed for the cabin with our rifles.

Dad opened the door.

"Well, there's them noon–day hunters now. How'd that old mountain treat you?" I recognized Whitey's voice before seeing his toothy tobacco–stained grin.

"Can't complain." Dad handed his rifle to John who stored them in the overhead rack on the ceiling of the back loft. "Melody got a handsome young buck with one shot and we carried all the meat down in a single trip."

"That so?" Whitey looked at me.

I walked past him and went to the back of the cabin where I unloaded my weapon and began cleaning it.

"Well, you folks must be plumb tuckered out. I'll be gettin' my old bones out of your way."

"Sure you won't stay? We're going to cut some fresh steak off that caribou." Dad washed his face and hands.

"No. Take a raincheck though. I'll be dropping by from time to time, I'm sure." Whitey stood up, positioned his trapper's hat and left the cabin with Dad and John.

"You didn't have to be so rude to him," Gay said.

I kept cleaning my rifle without bothering to answer.

CHAPTER 7
Whitey Returns

A chilling winter breeze rustled dead leaves on a birch tree as I stood at the ridge edge overlooking our field. The breeze worked its way through my heavy jacket. Arms folded, I squinted into falling dusk. Underfoot my feet stamped a fresh January snowfall into the smooth packed surface molded by weeks of this same afternoon vigilance. I wondered what was delaying Dad.

More than a month had passed since Sandra boarded the train on her 'Independence Day.' She left three weeks after I'd turned thirteen. Sandra and Gay had gone through a big fuss about my thirteenth birthday. I was really excited about finally becoming a teenager, but I wouldn't let Sandra know that. To me, being a teenager meant pimples and fighting with Mom. I didn't want any of that.

Right after Sandra had left, Dad started the trapline. His trail started from our cabin through the field to the Susitna River Bridge. He crossed the river then followed the tracks north to trap a beaver swamp at Mile 265. Continuing north, he would come out at Indian River, follow it upstream to the tracks, then come back via the hard packed railroad tracks until he reached mile 265 again. From there he went into the woods in the opposite direction, and still heading south, picked up a beaver swamp along the far bank of the Susitna River. He followed that swamp downstream until reaching a point where he was exactly opposite our cabin. Then he snowshoed across the river and came straight home through the field.

I'd walked the ten mile trapline with Dad several times. One time we'd made the river crossing in the dark. Following Dad's instructions, I had slipped out of my bindings and scooted my snowshoes along with only the toe strap on. I'd kept about fifty feet behind his lead when we started out across the still, snow–covered expanse. An open spot upstream bounced the echo of churning icy water off a small rock bluff somewhere behind us.

A shiver ran its way down my spine now as I listened to the same echo from deep river water. I concentrated on the area of field where I knew Dad would first appear and prayed he would make the crossing before full darkness.

"Is he coming?" Gay shouted from the cabin.

I gave one final squint. "Not yet."

"I'll pull the stew pot off the front of the stove then. It's scorching again." She went back inside.

Since Sandra had left, Gay cooked the meals and cleaned house most of the time. John and I helped a little, but Gay seemed to prefer taking charge. We'd also had more peace and quiet after my oldest sister left. She'd sent Christmas presents for all of us but when Mom came home for Christmas vacation, she made us send them back unopened. I was upset with Mom at first, but then got even more upset with Sandra, who had started this whole mess by wanting to get married at sixteen.

Gay seemed to adjust to Sandra's absence by spending a lot of time playing her flute. When she didn't play it, she polished it.

After a few minutes more of squinting in the darkness, I gave up my search for Dad and returned to the cabin.

"You want to eat now?" Gay questioned.

"No. I'll wait for Dad."

My stomach began to growl and I was just about to give in when I heard the sound of snowshoes being slapped together outside the cabin. Dad entered and I looked at him expectantly. But a bulging coat pocket produced only an unlucky gray jay which he put outside for future bait.

"What took you so long?" I asked over a bowl full of scorched stew.

"The river overflowed along the bank and across my packed trail. I had to go upstream and around it. It looks like a pretty large area of new ice will freeze up and it's as slick as glass. You kids better check it out."

Ever since Mom had given us ice skates for Christmas, we'd been looking for a good, large pond. We'd been using an area of the second slough. But the beaver in there had put his winter feed pile in the way so the rink was rather small.

When Dad left to check the trapline the next morning, we all pitched in with the dishes then took our shovels, ice pick, buckets and skates, and snowshoed down to the river's edge.

"This is great." John ran across the smooth surface, stopping suddenly to slide for several feet on his boots. "We don't even have to flood it."

Gay got out of her snowshoes and put a thermos of hot chocolate down on the blanket she'd carried with her. "Okay. Let's skate a little now, then flood the pond again so it stays nice and smooth."

John scooted his way back across the ice. My brother and I were up and skating before Gay, but when she did stand up and start circling the pond, I stopped to watch.

"How do you skate backwards like that?"

She moved away from me as quickly as I could go forwards.

"I don't know. I just turn around and push backwards is all." She did a mid–stride turn and began skating forwards again.

I stood still in the middle of the pond then tried to push back on the edges of my skates. The blades shaved little pieces of ice and my arches ached.

"Keep trying." Gay whisked by. "Relax a little."

I spent our whole ice skating period going only a half dozen yards backwards. Then, toes numb with cold, retreated to the edge of the pond and took off my skates.

"You're never going to learn that way." Gay skated up to me.

"I could do it if I really wanted. My feet are getting cold and besides I have school work back at the cabin to do."

Gay stood awhile looking at John who had been content to just circle the pond forwards concentrating on how fast he could go rather than style.

"My feet are cold too." Gay sat down on the blanket. "Let's flood the pond so when we come down tomorrow it will be nice and smooth again."

John raced towards us on his skates after Gay shouted to him. He turned sidewise and sprayed us with a layer of shaved ice. "I'll stay on my skates and carry the buckets. You two dig the hole."

My sister and I went to a corner, picked through the ice and handed John bucket after bucket of water. The air temperature was just right for flooding. Sometimes when it was too cold the water froze in fingers along the pond surface. That day it slid and settled without a ripple. We'd just finished the operation when Dad came past on his way home. Skates slung over our shoulders, we followed him back to the cabin. Whitey Rudder stood at the cabin door when we arrived.

"Well, c'mon in. What brings you down from Portage Creek?" Dad greeted.

"I didn't know I needed an excuse." Whitey took off his coat and hat, following us inside. "But now that you asked, a rain check on that caribou steak sounds good."

I looked straight at his toothy grin and didn't say a word.

"I guess we can manage that." Dad stoked up the firebox then placed the coffee pot up front on the stove.

"How's trapping been this year?" Dad pulled out a chair for himself while Gay started dinner.

"Oh fine, just fine. Had me a lot of fun with a wolverine."

John scooted his seat closer to the table but I turned and put my skates away.

"What do you mean?" My brother asked when Whitey seemed willing to let the subject drop.

"Now I'm right glad you asked that." He settled back in his chair and scratched at his black beard. "There was this here wolverine marauding my traps and I couldn't catch him because I didn't have any traps large enough to hold him. Them wolverine are strong, mean critters. Stubborn too. But I didn't know how stubborn until I rigged up something to keep this one busy so he'd leave the rest of my trapline alone."

"What did you do?" John asked as I sat down at the table.

"Well I took a moose head from one of my sets, one he'd been dragging away almost every day up this hill and over across the tundra, and rigged a little surprise for him." Whitey paused to accept a cup of coffee. He peeked over the rim at me with his dark eyes and I looked away.

"Well, one day I brought the head back and lashed a big round rock to it. I didn't even bother to set traps by it 'cause none of them would hold him anyway. The next time I went out to check my sets, that wolverine had packed a solid trail up the hill trying to get that moose head on top of the crest. But the moose head was still at the bottom.

"I said to myself, 'Whitey, you've got to hang around here and see what's goin' on.' So I set me up a camp a little ways from the kill and spied on him with binoculars. Sure enough that wolverine came back. He'd haul that head halfway up the hill, stop to rest, and then that boulder and head would come a' rollin' end over end back to the base."

Whitey motioned with his arms. "He's been working on that head all winter. I've got me one pooped wolverine up there. By the time he's finished playin' do–si–do with that moose head, I'll be able to hold him in a muskrat trap."

Whitey caught me looking at him now. "How've you two been doin' with your trapline this year?"

"We're not running one. Mom says we have to do our schoolwork." John made a face.

Whitey rubbed his beard. "Strikes me that there used to be a beaver down at the second slough. Have you tried to trap him yet?"

"We don't know how." John shrugged.

"Trappin' beaver is the easiest thing in the world to do, once you get to him. I'll show you if you want." He paused, looking at Dad. "That is if it's all right."

"Sure." Dad helped Gay set the table.

"You be ready bright and early tomorrow morning then. We'll need a shovel, an axe, something to dig through the ice with and some #2 snares."

"We don't have any snares," I said.

"Well it just so happens I brought some down from the Portage." Whitey accepted the caribou steak, grinning. "You two just be ready tomorrow morning."

CHAPTER 8
To Catch a Beaver

Between the time Whitey left that afternoon and the next morning, John and I had been down to the second slough several times. We shoveled off different areas of ice around the alder feed pile. That was where Whitey found us.

"With all the diggin' you two have done, did you find a spot with a lot of air bubbles in the ice?" Whitey put the snares down next to our shovels.

"Yeah. Right over there." John pointed.

Whitey jumped down off the mound of snow we'd piled up and onto the thick layer of ice.

"Yep. This looks like where he's been travelin' all right. Let's start diggin' a hole about two foot square right here."

John ran to the shovels, pulled out the axe and ice pick and came back.

"You can tell this is a live house 'cause you saw the beaver making a feed pile in here last winter. But do you know how to tell it's live once the snow has covered up that feed pile?" Whitey looked at me.

I shook my head.

"C'mon. I'll show you." He traipsed without snowshoes up to the top of the house, then bent down. "You see way back down under them branches?" He pointed. "Where those long ice crystals are? Those crystals tell you there's heat in that house. If there's heat, there's beaver. That's why wolverine always go straight to the top of a beaver house. They can smell 'em in there. 'Course we're the only ones that can get to 'em." Whitey grinned and stood up. "Good place for a wolverine set is always right on top of a live beaver house."

John had started to chip out the ice and we returned to watch.

"Make sure you keep the edges square now. You're gonna tend to chip that hole out smaller and smaller. But if you keep it nice and square from the beginning you won't have water a'splashin' up at you while you try to trim it out." He jumped down to the ice again. "Here, let me chop for awhile."

Whitey chopped with quick sound strokes. Soon we had a square hole in the two-foot thick ice. Following his instructions, John cut a dry spruce pole about four inches in diameter and six feet long. Then Whitey sent him back for some green willow poles. I watched as Whitey placed the spruce pole across the hole. He fastened the ends of two snares to it a couple feet apart from one another. Then he picked up the willows and began to cut small nicks out of the bark with the hand axe.

"If you do this in a few places, the beaver can see it better. After four months of eating those waterlogged branches he stored up last fall, this is going to smell just like dessert." The trapper drew the back of his mittened hand across his nose. "That's when we spring our little surprise."

Whitey made a large loop out of one of the snares now and dipped it into the water. He set the other snare on the opposite side of the bait sticks which he had previously jabbed into the silty bottom of the slough. Then he stood up and climbed out of the hole.

"If you don't want to dig that out each day to check your snares, just put some green spruce boughs over it and pack a little snow on top. That will help the ice freeze clear and thin. Then all you'll have to do is come down, take the boughs off and peer through the ice." Whitey cupped his hands around his face.

"If the snares are still set, leave things be. If they've been tripped, take them out and reset them. And if you've got a beaver," Whitey paused, grinning, "take him out too."

The sourdough slipped into his snowshoes. "Brought you a couple of extra snares just in case you want to make another set."

We thanked Whitey and watched him snowshoe away. John went into the nearby woods for some spruce boughs while I waited by the set. When he returned be began covering the set as Whitey described.

"You'd better get to work if you want a set of your own. This one's mine."

"No, it's not. Whitey made it for both of us."

"Whitey and I made it. You just hung around and listened. So go somewhere else and make another one." John continued piling the branches. "Besides, with two sets we'll have twice the chance of catching the beaver."

"Okay, mister smarty pants. I will make my own set. I don't need you or Whitey Rudder, or anyone else to help me either." I picked up the shovel and began walking away. "And I don't want you coming near it either."

John finished the final touches on the first set before I'd cleared away a spot for mine.

"See you back at the cabin." He put his shoes on and left me alone.

Using Whitey's set as an example, I tried to remember everything he'd said. A few hours later I had my own set and covered it with spruce boughs.

The next morning John and I kept an eye on one another. Then after breakfast we both left the cabin together to check the sets. As Whitey had predicted, the ice had formed into a thick clear sheet of glass and I got my face right up to it, looking down into the water for my snares. They were still there, set and ice free. I sat back on my knees debating whether or not to chop out the layer of fresh ice. Across from me John began whacking energetically at his set.

"Did you get him?" I ran over.

"I think so. I couldn't see the snares because of all the bubbles in the ice. That must mean he's caught."

A few whacks cleared the hole of ice and John pulled on the snares. They came up quickly. What remained of the bait pole bobbed up and down in the water. John grabbed it, staring at the chewed end.

"He took the bait and got away."

"Well, at least he came over to your set. He didn't even bother with mine."

"But how could he get away? Whitey made the set."

I shrugged.

John jabbed the chewed bait pole into the shoveled snow bank and climbed out of the hole. I waited for my brother to return from the nearby willows with his new bait and watched him remake the set.

In the next few weeks I learned that beaver trapping was not as easy as Whitey had led us to believe. Both of us became victims of stolen bait and tripped snares. One time John thought he had the beaver. But it turned out he'd snared another willow length which the animal had probably been carrying back to its house to eat. John worked half the day trying to free the snare without damaging it. Another time I'd set my snare too big and must have caught the beaver by its powerful tail. He finally managed to slip free but not before kinking one of my snares into a corkscrew. Down to one snare against John's two, I lost most hope of being the one to catch our elusive prey. But, one day in early February I looked into my plate glass ice window and saw a clawed, webbed foot.

"It's the beaver," I yelled to John. "Give me the hatchet."

John jumped into the hole next to me. "Careful you don't cut him."

I heard John and kept hacking. As soon as the hole was big enough we both hauled my catch out.

"He's huge." John unstrapped the cord of the packboard he'd brought along.

"It's my catch. I want to pack it." I picked the beaver up by its scaly tail, half dragging the heavy animal out of the hole.

John gave me the packboard and I cinched the beaver down tightly. Then he helped me load the pack.

Gay cleared her books away when, back at the cabin, we deposited the load on the table. Then we sat and waited for Dad to come home from the trapline.

All I knew about beaver skinning was what Whitey had talked about. Stretched properly it looked like a big circle. By measuring first from nose to tail, then left to right and adding the two amounts together, you'd come up with the size and value of the pelt. If the total was below sixty-five inches the size was regular. Sixty-five or better meant a blanket. Seventy-two or better made it a super blanket. Looking at my catch, I felt certain it fell into the super category, but didn't know how to even begin to find that out.

We watched by kerosene lamplight that night as Dad made a slit in the fur from the base of the beaver's tail, up the belly and to the chin. Then with his instructions we all helped skin the fur off in one huge piece. Carcass cleaned and packed safely away in a snowbank for a future dinner, we began looking for a place to stretch the hide.

The only area large enough turned out to be our door. After Dad drew a circle in red crayon, he tacked the hide to it. When the tacking was done, my pelt looked more oblong than round because the door was too narrow to take up the full width of the fur. But nonetheless, the pelt totaled seventy-five inches. I spent most that night sitting crosslegged on the floor next to the pelt, carefully fleshing off excess fat and gristle.

CHAPTER 9
In The Traces

The pelt took several weeks to dry. When we removed it from the door a permanent red circle, perforated with tack marks and stained by beaver grease, remained. During the time the pelt dried, I'd taught myself how to skate backwards. Then one day when both Gay and John had gone ice skating and Dad was on the trapline, we again had an unexpected visit from Whitey. I proudly displayed my fur.

"Boy, that's a nice one." Whitey took the hide, examining both the fur and skinning job. "Nice prime fur and a good job cleaning too. Ought to bring top dollar at the Rendezvous."

"Next year I'm going to trap beaver from those swamps Dad has on his trapline trail."

"That so?" Whitey looked at me. "Them swamps can be tricky. Sometimes they don't freeze tight."

"I can handle them."

Whitey handed the pelt back to me and I rolled it, tying a piece of heavy twine around the middle. "Then with the money for the furs I can buy some big traps to catch wolverine."

"Wolverine," Whitey snorted. "Them's a critter that shouldn't be messed with. They can get real ornery when they're trapped. In fact they're downright ornery without being trapped."

I shrugged and tossed my pelt on one of the bunks. "Doesn't bother me. I can be just as ornery."

The sourdough scratched his beard. "Might not hurt to have someone help you learn how to handle a trapline that size on your own."

"I can learn by myself. That's how I learn everything else."

"Yeah, I don't doubt that you could." Whitey looked at the stained door then stood up abruptly. "Well, I've got to catch the train back to Portage and shut down my camp. You be at the station house a week from now and I'll drop some of my old traps off for you. They're not much, and they won't hold wolverine, but if you're serious about trapping you're gonna have to get staked somehow."

"You're really going to do that?"

"Sure. You've got to share with your brother though."

"That's okay. I don't mind."

"All right then. I'll see you next week." He adjusted his trapper's cap. "Be sure you're at the train 'cause I'm just gonna drop them off, then me and my dogs are heading for Talkeetna."

"I'll be there," I promised.

All three of us kids were at the station when the train pulled to a stop that next week. As promised, Whitey threw off a gunny sack of traps. Then he untied one of the half-dozen dogs that milled around on their chains in the baggage car and threw the end of the heavy leash to us. A big black dog with pale blue eyes leapt the five-foot drop to the ground without hesitation.

"That there's my lead dog Spook." Whitey motioned. "He's taught me everything I know. But he's gettin' a little too old to keep up with the younger dogs. Should be just what you kids need to start your own dog team."

We held tightly to the chain as the train picked up speed and Whitey shouted the rest of his advice. "Sometimes Spook needs a little straightenin' out but generally he knows what he's doin'. If you listen to him, he'll larn you a few things."

The big husky sat with an uninterested look in his pale blue eyes while the train passed by. Then we all gathered around petting and talking to the huge, thickly-furred animal. Spook remained aloof for a few minutes, then finally the tip of his great black tail began to wag. He needed little coaxing to follow us home.

We worked closely with the dog for the next week. Whitey had supplied a harness and tow line which, boiled first, was attached to the traces of a small homemade toboggan. It didn't take me long to figure out why Whitey got rid of the dog. Spook was a bagful of tricks. He'd often balk at pulling a load, pretending it was too heavy. Or he'd develop a sudden limp. Or, get the sled going full tilt down a hill then jump off to the side and brace himself. The toboggan would whisk past, jerk to an abrupt stop and send me flying out into the snow. Then as I'd stand up wiping myself off and reading him the riot act, Spook would lie down, look at me with those huge pale blue eyes and begin nibbling at the snow.

For Spook's more playful days in harness, a threat with a green willow switch usually turned him serious enough to get down to the job at hand. In a few extra days time the lead dog seemed to have resigned himself to letting kids be the boss and we felt our dog team for the next season was well on the way.

One morning in March when the late-morning sun peeked over the mountain's crest and shined into my eyes through the back cabin window, I looked down from my bunk to see Dad still in bed. He was usually on the trapline by that time.

"Aren't you going out today?"

"No. I don't feel well. The trapline is going to have to pass."

"Can I go?"

"No. It's too late. You couldn't get home before the crust on the snow starts getting soft."

"I'll take Spook." I jumped down from the bunk pulling on my jeans. "With him pulling me I'll be back in no time."

Dad paused a few minutes. "Okay. But be sure you cross the river on the snowshoe trail under the bridge, not over it. I don't want you caught with that sled on those tracks if a train comes by."

"I want to go too." John sat up.

"No. Just one of you can go. Spook can't pull the both of you if the snow gets soft."

I went outside before John could talk Dad into letting him come, and quickly hitched up Spook. Minutes later we swished off down the trail. Dad had been wrong. The snow was ice hard on our trail and Spook began to gallop. I stood up in the toboggan keeping balance with a single rein fastened to the front of the sled. Spook seemed eager to exercise and we bounced down the trail reaching the bridge in a short fifteen minutes. I guided Spook to Dad's trail across the frozen river. He followed the weaving trapline trail up and down huge chunks of snow-covered ice that had piled up from an early winter jam. Although these mid-winter shifts of ice were rare, they came on suddenly for reasons I never understood. It was as if an entire area of river ice buckled and heaved under a restless, icy current, anxious to shed the grip of winter. Then the jumbled ice cakes would lock solid in the refrozen surface and be covered under a fresh white blanket of snow. As I bumped my way over them I mused how they looked as harmless as giant, melting marshmallows.

When we'd covered half the barren trapline, I stopped to give Spook a rest and started working on a half-frozen apple. Spook lay in the snow, a warm early afternoon sun glistened off his thick black coat as he nibbled delicately at a small piece of Limburger cheese I'd been using for scent. I'd surrendered the delicacy to him for being a good dog. We'd made excellent time. Spook, in his congenial mood, hadn't needed any 'straightening out' and again jumped up readily on my command.

But when we started this time, the persistent sun had begun melting the crust. It stuck in large globs to the metal toboggan bottom, forcing me to walk. I sank past my ankles in the soft trail. By the time we had covered the last beaver swamp and reached the river crossing, dusk fell rapidly around us. With only a mile to go, I urged Spook ahead onto the level snow-covered ice. Spook was eager to get home too, and seeming to sense the cabin ahead, started out with a bound. Then, only a slight way out, the dog stopped short. I tripped, falling hard on my knees into the toboggan.

"Get up, Spook," I commanded.

He stood rigid, ears forward.

"C'mon Spook. This is no time for games." I trudged to the front and pulled at his harness.

Spook stood solid, wrestling against me. I turned and studied the path in front of us. There was nothing wrong with it. I could see Dad's packed trail clearly to the other bank of the river several hundred yards distant. I returned to the toboggan and picked up the willow switch from inside, beating it threateningly against the wooden bottom. Spook still refused my order, so I struck him across the ribs with my weapon. He jumped sidewise, not taking the punishing blow. The dog's ears were flattened now, eyes big, but he held his ground.

"What's the matter with you?" I looked out onto the trail across the river. There was no sign of melt or open water anywhere. "The ice is safe."

To prove my point, I started out ahead of him, traveling fifty feet or so onto the frozen surface. I was halfway tempted to just walk in front of him all the way across to show him everything was all right. But instead I turned and began jumping up and down. "See?" I yelled.

The dog stood still, ears forward. He looked upstream and down.

Then, feet fidgeting, he whined slightly.

I knelt down clapping my hands together. "C'mon boy, it's okay. Honest."

Spook made a move forward, but then whirled around. The empty sled dragged broadside a few seconds before flipping back onto the trail headed the opposite direction. Spook began a loping pace back into the woods with me running behind.

"Whoa! Whoa!" I yelled.

In less than a hundred yards I found the dog alongside the trail. He had waded up to his midriff in deep woodland snow, where he nonchalantly sampled the melting white while eyeing my approach.

"Spook." I said threateningly as I trudged closer, sinking farther in the melting snow than I had only a few scant minutes before.

Spook's white eyes widened. His ears flattened. He let me come within several feet of the tie–off rope dragging behind the sled then jumped back onto the path and moved ahead just fast enough to keep the trailing rope from my grasp. If I sped up, he sprinted. If I stopped, he stopped. Each step took us further down the trail away from home.

By the time Spook finally dragged the toboggan off the trapline trail and back onto the railroad tracks at Mile 265, we were several miles north of the Susitna River Bridge and it was dark. I flogged him soundly with the switch, then ordered him home. Too tired to walk anymore, I laid down in the sled. Then later I awoke from my daydream to the thump of the toboggan as it bumped over the bare railroad ties of the Susitna River Bridge.

I jumped up and out of the sled, running alongside in the dark, urging Spook ahead with haste. Without my weight, Spook covered the several hundred yard expanse quickly. I didn't argue with him when he started pulling the toboggan home by the railroad tracks instead of going down the side of the bank to pick up the field road home. The next time the sled stopped we were in front of the cabin.

Leaving Spook still hitched up I entered. A lamp burned low on the table but no one was there. I went back outside.

"Dad! Gay! John!" I called.

Hearing nothing, I unhooked Spook's harness and slipped him out of it. Tail between his legs, the dog disappeared inside his house. I chastised him one final time while snapping the chain to his collar.

Again calling out for my missing family members, I walked over to the ridge edge and spotted several lantern lights bobbing back and forth half-way across the field.

"Dad!" I shouted through cupped hands.

The lantern movement stopped. Then one swayed back and forth in signal. I ran down the ridgeside trapline trail towards them but upon reaching the edge of the field sank knee deep in slush. Dragging my legs free, I scrambled to the base of the ridge and waited. The lanterns came closer. Dad led, his snowshoes dragging with wet dirty snow.

"Where the hell have you been?" A flickering lantern revealed his pale face.

"Spook wouldn't cross the river." Dad shook the words out of me and I began to cry. "Then he ran away and I had to chase him all the way back to Mile 265. We took the tracks home instead of the river crossing."

"Oh, thank God." Dad clutched me close. "Thank God."

"What happened?" I wiped my eyes.

"An ice jam, just before dark." Gay pointed her lantern back down the trail. Now I saw huge ice cakes and cottonwood logs in the expanse behind her. "It blocked the water above the ice skating pond and the river came right through our field."

A few minutes later, the four of us crested the small ridge back to the cabin. Spook sat outside his house, ears again forward. His pale blue eyes shined like two fire-red coals in the reflecting lantern light. The big dog watched us for a few seconds then released a loud yawn combined with a casual stretch, and crawled back into his house.

Instead of following the others inside, I walked over to the dog house. The huge black head poked out from the opening as I approached. Inside, his tail beat a meek rhythm against the walls. I squatted down and sat petting him for a long time.

CHAPTER 10
A Real Thorn

    Crystalized snow sprayed ahead with each forward movement of my huge Army surplus bunny boots as I led our small procession up the section house trail. I watched the flashlight's beam make snow granules glitter like a field of diamonds in front of me. Minutes later I stood on the section house boardwalk toying with the light's reflections while waiting for the passenger train.
    Gay and I were going to town to visit the Ihlys and Mom. But most important, I wanted to sell my beaver pelt. I shifted the rolled up fur under my arm now thinking about the stash of money left in my piggy bank at the cabin. Mom had sent Gay and me each a crisp ten dollar bill bill to spend, so I'd left the rest of my savings at home. Gay hadn't been as conservative.
    Feeling for the greenback folded neatly in the breast pocket of my heavy work shirt, I thought about how to spend it as I continued to sweep the light back and forth over the frozen sparkling snow. Soon bored with that, I walked a short distance from the others and lay prone in an undisturbed field of white. Here the snow had fed on warmer March days and cold starlit skies to form surface crystals which grew healthily into towering spires. I brought my face level with the ground and looked into a miniature frozen forest caught in the prism of light.
    "What are you doing? You'll get your good clothes all wet." Gay came up beside me.
    "I was looking at the frost. It's really pretty over here."
    "You'd better come back to the tracks. Dad and John thought they heard the train."
    Reluctantly, I stood. Sparkles fell from my clothes, tinkling like chimes around my feet as I walked a careful path back to the section house where the others waited. The night– cold, dark and silent, made a perfect backdrop for the northern lights which we watched as they danced across the stars. Soon a lonely whistle flowed lazily down our valley. No doubt it continued miles down the tracks, reaching others who stood waiting like ourselves. The train rounded the north bend before John stepped between the rails with the flashlight.

"Tell Mom 'hi' for us." Dad hugged me when I handed him the flashlight. Squealing brakes kept me from hearing anything more and both Gay and I waved our final goodbye through billowing clouds of warm brake air released into sub-zero cold. Then I mounted the vestibule behind my older sister and waited as she opened a heavy metal door leading into the passenger car. The rush of warm air over my chilled body was welcome.

Our car was empty. So while the train gathered speed, I chose a nearby window seat. Beaver pelt occupying the seat next to me, I peeled off my outer clothes and sat down to watch darkness rush past the mirror image next to me. Gay sat down across the aisle from me, doing the same. Occasionally I caught a glimpse of the engine light ahead. It searched the path and led the rest of its dark caterpillar body around a bend. Each segment swayed squeakily back and forth in an independent rhythm.

Our conductor dimmed the lights and I sat back. I wanted to sleep most of the five hour train ride so that when we arrived in Anchorage the following morning I wouldn't miss a moment of the city's luxuries. Mom said we could eat all the ice cream we wanted while we visited. And the Ihlys had a television too. There were also movies to go to, shops to browse in and most important to me, hardware stores. I hoped to buy some traps with the money from my beaver pelt.

My mind wandered to television now and whether or not it was black and white or color. I'd never seen a color television. We'd left San Francisco before color television sets were 'state of the art', or at least that's what Dad had told us back then. And now, even if we had a generator for power on the homestead, Dad explained that we couldn't get television pictures because the surrounding mountains stopped the line-of-sight transmission from reaching us. I remembered hearing, although too tired to think of where, that at one time someone in Gold Creek had climbed Disappointment Mountain and erected a small metal TV antenna on its crest. But a powerful tundra wind twisted and blew the antenna away.

Television fell into the same luxury category as hot running water, indoor plumbing and lights that turned on with the flick of a finger. Now, while listening to the constant clickity-clack of the train wheels under me, I made a mental note that city toilets needed flushing, then settled into my seat.

"You girls are growing up faster than I can keep track of you." The conductor stopped on his way past. "One's already gone and from the looks of it, it won't be long before Gold Creek will lose another one."

Gay sat up in her seat, smiling.

"Just don't let any young buck rush you into anything when the time comes," the conductor continued. "This state already has its quota of child–brides."

"I'll be careful." Gay crossed her heart.

"And what about you?" He directed his attention my way. "Have any confirmed bachelor in mind?"

"I'm never leaving the homestead." I straightened my beaver pelt.

"The eligible girls in the bush are few and far between." The conductor looked back at Gay. "They hardly get a chance to crawl out of the cradle before some trapper steals 'em away to some cabin in the hills."

"I already live in a cabin in the hills," I said. "Nobody's going to have to steal me away to do that."

The conductor laughed. "I wouldn't want to be the one that has to wrestle you away from the cradle. You're going to be a real thorn in some poor fellow's hide." He tipped his blue hat then continued down the aisle.

"What are you going to spend your money on?" I asked my sister.

"I don't know. I'll find something, though." She turned from the window. "Are you hungry?"

"Yeah. How much longer before we get to Anchorage?"

"A long time. Let's go back to the dining car and have breakfast. It'll help pass the time."

I followed her lead through several cars like our own with their scattered sleeping passengers. I had trouble negotiating the beaver fur past the small bolted–down cocktail tables in the club car. When we finally reached the dining car Gay sat down at one of the tables.

"Do you have to carry that thing every place you go?" She watched as I pulled out the chair next to me and stood my pelt on it.

"I don't want anyone to steal it."

"Nobody's going to steal it. You could have left it on the overhead rack back in our car."

"I feel better when it's with me."

A waitress weaved her way towards us. "Would you like some coffee?" She stood braced on spraddled legs, swaying with the train.

"Yes. Please." Gay turned her cup over and I followed suit.

The waitress left and returned shortly with breakfast menus and a coffee pot. Then she stood weaving while we looked at the breakfast selection.

I peered over the top of the huge menu. "Are the eggs fresh?"

The waitress shrugged, jaw working rhythmically at a piece of gum.

"For that price they should be fresh," I mumbled and looked back down. "Do you get free coffee when you order a complete breakfast?" I looked up again.

"Coffee is twenty cents with or without breakfast," she said.

"What about refills? Are they free?" I put my menu down and Gay kicked me under the table.

"Refills are ten cents each." The waitress leaned over awkwardly. "Are you ready to order now?"

In a few seconds I watched our waitress sway back to the kitchen.

"You're embarrassing me to tears," Gay hissed. "What do you mean 'Are the eggs fresh?'"

"If I'm going to pay that price for an egg I don't want it to be out of cold storage. I eat enough of those at home. And imagine paying for refills on coffee. This isn't even full to begin with." I looked down at the jiggling contents of my heavy ceramic cup.

"They don't fill it all the way so it doesn't spill."

"If they're going to give you a half cup they should only charge for a half cup."

"Be quiet, will you! People are looking at us!"

"Let them look. I don't care."

"Well, I do. So just be quiet."

I picked up my coffee and took several large swallows, draining it. "It's only lukewarm, too," I muttered.

My eggs weren't fresh. I could tell by the way the pale flat yolks stared up at me. Only Gay's warning stare kept me from saying anything. And barely full but two dollars poorer, I headed back with her to my seat.

"That's the last time I eat there. I'm going to pack food from home next time."

"If you had brought more money you wouldn't have had to break that ten dollar bill yet."

"If I have to spend my money on rotten eggs, I'm glad I left the rest at home."

"They weren't rotten," Gay said, taking her seat.

We didn't talk much the rest of the trip, and when the train pulled into the busy Anchorage depot, Gay put on her coat, hurriedly unboarding. I took my time positioning my trapper's hat much like Whitey's. Then, pelt again tucked under one arm, I headed out the car and onto the platform. Gay already waited beside the Ihlys and Mom. I held the pelt between my legs while giving Mom a tight hug.

"Welcome to the big city," Mrs. Ihly greeted and Mr. Ihly nodded. A grin spread across his face as he looked at me. "Is there anything special you kids would like to do while you're here?"

"I'd like to see Sandra," Gay said. "She wrote me her phone number."

"I want to watch television with a great big bowl of ice cream in front of me," I said.

"I'm afraid there isn't much on TV during the day." We followed the Ihlys to their car as Mrs. Ihly spoke. I had barely noticed the sounds of traffic around me. "But tonight we should be able to see some good shows."

"You kids can do some window shopping until then," Mom said. "I've got to get back to work, but I'll meet you at the Ihlys tonight for supper."

We all piled into the car and Mr. Ihly drove Mom back to the house where she worked. When we got to the Ihlys' house I remembered to take my boots off on the porch before going inside. In the living room was a large TV.

"You children are welcome to stay around the house or go downtown. It's about nine blocks away." Mrs. Ihly took off her coat and scarf.

"How far is that?" I asked.

"About as far as from your place to Botner's," Mr. Ihly said.

"Can I go now?"

"Sure. See that street in front of the house? Just keep walking down it until you come to 4th Avenue, then turn right. In a few more blocks you'll be in downtown Anchorage."

"I guess I should go with you so you don't get lost," Gay sighed.

"I won't get lost. I'll just blaze the telephone poles so I can find my way back here whenever I want." I smiled but a worried look crossed Mrs. Ihly's face.

"I think it would be better if you used a map." She began searching through a dining bureau drawer. "Once you get a general idea of how the city is laid out you won't have any trouble."

"I was only kidding about blazing telephone poles." I suddenly felt embarrassed.

"Just the same, I think a map would come in handy." She produced the folded piece of paper. "I'll write our telephone number up here on the corner in case you need to reach us."

"Where are all the fur buyers?" I looked at the expanded map.

"Look in the phone book, silly." Gay dialed a number from a letter she'd recently received from Sandra.

"I was going to do that next." I walked over, picked up the book and with Mr. Ihly's help found several furriers within the downtown area.

Then, map and addresses in my jeans hip pocket, I went out on the porch, cinched up my boots and picked up my pelt.

"Are you sure you don't want to come?" I looked back at Gay.

"No. Sandra said she'd be by and we'd go downtown together. I'll probably run into you there."

"Tell her not to go out of her way on my account." I put my hat in place and closed the door behind me. Mom was still mad at Sandra, that was a good enough reason for me to be mad at her too.

Aware of the traffic noises now, I began walking towards downtown. Snow along the gutters and on the walks was a frozen dirty gray and in my slippery–bottomed bunny boots I had a difficult time keeping balance. I walked slowly until reaching the cross street sign saying 4th Avenue, then turned right as Mr. Ihly had directed.

Both sides of the street in front of me were crammed tightly with small stores, restaurants and cars. I stood on a corner watching the congested traffic for a few seconds, deciding what to do first. Several people in business suits passed widely by me as I pulled out my slip of paper and saw that the first furrier was only two blocks away. It was difficult to pass by all the store front displays and the few minutes walk turned out to take a little longer than I had originally planned. As I paused looking into one window, I heard several people behind me stop and exchange a few words. Only one made me tune my ears into the conversation and that was 'homesteader'. When I turned, they exchanged glances and departed.

    I looked carefully into the large plate glass window. My skinny blue jean clad legs came out of gigantic 'alley–oop' boots. The belt holding my pants up was several sizes too big and I'd doubled the end back through some of the loops a second time. But I knew it was the beaver pelt I carried tightly under my arm that attracted the attention. I tucked in my shirt and zipped up my cloth coat. Then I repositioned the rolled pelt for maximum exposure and again began my walk toward the furrier's shop.

CHAPTER 11
The City

A bell tinkled when I opened the door. Inside, furs spilled from racks and bins. I saw no one in the shop at first. Then a head peered over a mound of pelts in the kind of half loft area of the shop.

"What do you want?" The balding head asked.

"I want to sell my fur."

"Beaver aren't bringing a good price this year." He heaved his overweight body down a runged ladder, breathing heavily.

"I see some right here." I touched a mound of pelts. They were soft, not stiff like mine.

"Those are tanned. They cost more. Are you buying or selling?"

"I'm selling." I backed away from the rich-looking furs.

"Let's see what you've got then. I don't have all day."

Quickly now I untied my fur. The man took it from me. He rubbed his fingers through the fur. Then he flipped the hide over, eyes squinting.

"It's not a very good pelt."

"What's wrong with it?" I moved closer.

"Well." The man hesitated. "For one thing it's stretched wrong. It should be in more of a circle." He motioned with his hands. "And it's too dark. We like to buy beaver with a lighter color."

"Oh." I began rolling up the pelt.

"Tell you what though." He wiped the sweat beads off his shiny head. "I'll give you seven dollars for it."

I paused a moment, then continued rolling. "I'll come back later if I decide to sell," I said, retying the bundle.

"Seven dollars will buy a lot of candy." The man rubbed his hands together.

I smiled as politely as I could, put the fur under my arm and shook my head.

"We're closing early today, so don't take too long to change your mind," the man warned.

As I closed the shop door, the bell tinkled behind me.

I'd been hoping for twenty dollars or more for my pelt and now traveled a little slower to the next shop. There a thin man with a serious look on his face handled my pelt, rubbing his hand through the short fur.

"I know it's a little darker than the usual pelt," I apologized.

"There's nothing wrong with the color. It's a nice color." He flipped the fur over. "It's a good job of skinning too. But I can't give you premium price for it."

"Because of the way it's stretched?" I asked.

"No. That will be reshaped when it's tanned. We bought all the beaver we needed during the Fur Rendezvous. The market is glutted now."

"You're selling that one over there for forty dollars. It's not as big as this one or even tanned." I pointed.

The man smiled. "You're right. But you see, right now I'm buying your fur, not selling it."

"What does that matter? It's still worth forty dollars."

"Not to me. To me your pelt is worth ten dollars at the most."

I brushed the fur of my pelt back into place with my hand. "Well, it's worth forty dollars to me." I knew I was fighting tears.

The man shrugged. "Then you should keep it." He went back to the job of sorting furs.

I stood, pelt in hand, watching him throw a small fur into a pile to the left, another to the right. Then slowly and carefully I rerolled my pelt, tying it with the piece of rope.

"Twelve dollars, tops," the man said as I turned to go out the door. "You won't get a better offer."

I shook my head and left.

The noises of the city irritated me now. I stopped at several more furriers for the same story. Then stomach growling, I went into a department store. Pelt held between my shins, I sat at the fountain and ordered a jumbo banana split. I took my time eating the dessert at the crowded counter. Several times someone next to me bumped their feet against my boots and I tried desperately to squeeze them into as small a space possible in front of me. At the end of my meal I asked for a cup of coffee and the busy waitress whisked by with the pot giving me a 'restaurant' size cupful. I paid a dollar for my food, decided against a tip, then picked up my pelt and went back out on the noisy sidewalk.

The walk home seemed intolerably long. My feet ached from traveling hard sidewalks. I tried not to think about how much farther it was to the Ihlys' house. Instead, my thoughts turned to how I could get traps for next year's trapping season. Twelve dollars would only buy a few large traps, not enough to run a full line of wolverine sets. I'd also been disappointed to see how much wolverine and beaver parkas cost. Our family would never be able to afford parkas out of a store like other people. But maybe if John and I could trap all the fur necessary for the parkas, we could have them made. Animals we caught and skinned other than wolverine and beaver could be used as partial payment towards the cost of construction.

What I had to do now was figure out a way to get the traps we needed for wolverine without selling any of the furs. We had enough smaller traps, and beaver snares weren't very expensive. But large traps were. I held onto my pelt even tighter now, knowing we'd made a start towards the parkas I had in mind.

I was up early the next morning ready to head back downtown, this time to spend my remaining seven dollars. We would be going home on the next morning's train so that day was my last chance to window-shop.

This time Gay didn't wait for Sandra to call. Instead she left with me for 4th Avenue right after we had finished the breakfast dishes. I hadn't had much time to window shop the day before and now every store we entered we stayed in until the storekeepers began looking nervous.

Gay was dressed a lot like me except her faded jeans weren't baggy around her legs and she didn't need a belt to cinch up the waist. By early afternoon she'd taken off her coat and rolled up the sleeves of her lumberjack shirt which tucked neatly into her pants. By the time we entered the Army-Navy surplus store still looking for something to buy, I noticed we were getting a lot of looks from young men.

A display case near the cash register caught my eye and my big boots clumped on the plank floor as I walked over to it. "Hey, Gay, c'mere," I motioned excitedly.

Gay glided over to me.

"Look." I pointed. "Isn't it beautiful?" The display cabinet held a variety of side and pocket knives but I pointed to one sideknife with a bone handle.

"How much is this one?" I asked the young cashier who'd come over to the counter

"That's six dollars and ninety five cents," he said.

"I'll take it." I whipped the bills out of my pocket. Gay stood nearby.

"I'm sorry. That's a display model. It's the only one we have left."

"I don't mind. I'll take it anyway."

"No. You don't understand." He shook his head, a silly grin on his face. "I can't take any of the knives out of the display case. We have the particular knife on order, though. It should be in stock again in a few weeks."

"But I'm going back home tomorrow." I held out my money.

"I'm sorry. It's store policy," he continued shaking his head. "Besides, I don't even have a key to the display case. I can take an order for you, though, and mail one to you."

"No. I'll just look around for something else, I guess." I crumpled the money and pocketed it.

I breezed through the remaining shelves while Gay still stood by the counter, talking to the cashier.

"You coming?" I said on my way out.

"No. I want to look around some more. I'll see you back at the Ihlys' house."

"Okay," I shrugged.

The few remaining stores had nothing like the knife. But I wanted to bring something home to show Dad and John. I had picked up several different trinkets at a couple of stores and carried them halfway to watchful cashiers before changing my mind. Finally, I decided to head for home empty–handed.

On my way back I passed a hardware store with a large display window I hadn't seen before. There were a variety of traps and snares in the window. One held the heavily furred paw of a mounted wolverine. It stood with its back arched up like a cat. Its thin black lips were curled back in a frothy snarl. I studied the trap on the animal's foot, then went inside.

"Is that a #4 on that wolverine?" I asked.

"No. It's a #3." The clerk looked up at me from an inventory list.

"Will a #3 hold a wolverine?"

"Sure. It's a little smaller in jaw size. But it's just as strong."

"May I see one?"

"Sure. They're right over there." He tilted his head toward the back of the store, then returned to study the list in front of him.

I walked over to some traps that hung by their chains from large spikes driven into a solid wood wall. I took a double–spring #4 off the wall first and put it on the floor. Then standing on each spring with my heels, I bent down and tried to force the jaws apart.

"Careful. Those things aren't toys, you know." The clerk came over to me just as the trap springs slipped from under my heels, sending the trap skidding.

The clerk winced. "Are you okay?"

"Yeah." I felt my face getting warm, so didn't look at him as I recovered the trap, rehung it and repeated the procedure successfully with a #3 trap.

"How much does a #4 cost?" I asked still holding the sprung #3.

"Eight dollars and fifty cents."

"What about this one?" I extended the trap.

"A double–spring #3 will cost you seven dollars even."

"I'll take it." I began wrapping the chain around one of the springs.

"Whatever for?"

"Wolverine."

He took the trap from me now, staring. Then a clearness came into his eyes.

"You must be a homesteader!" The clerk smiled. "Just be careful you don't come off your trapline wearing one of these things as a bracelet," he warned as he rung up the purchase.

Gay was already back at the house talking to Sandra on the phone when I got back. I headed straight for the basement where I practiced setting the strong trap. Then when Mom came for supper I put my trap next to the beaver pelt and headed upstairs.

"Sandra said she and Doug are moving up to Chulitna in a few weeks." Gay sat down at the table.

"I thought she didn't like it in the bush." Mrs. Ihly served up the meal while Mom busied herself passing plates.

"Oh, no. Sandra loves Chulitna. Doug showed it to her right after the wedding. They have a nice log home on a lake and a beautiful view of Mt. McKinley."

"I guess a view makes all the difference in the world," Mom said.

"Did you girls find anything to buy today?" Mr. Ihly sat down in front of a full plate.

"I got a #3 trap. It's really strong and the man said it would hold a wolverine as well as a #4."

"What about you, Gay?"

"I got a beautiful sideknife." She got up from the table, went over to a package and brought the knife back.

"How did you get that? The clerk said he wouldn't sell it."

"Sometimes boys say a lot of things they don't really mean." Gay winked.

"Gay, you shouldn't do things like that." Mom filled my glass with milk.

"It was harmless." Gay tossed the knife onto the couch then sat down.

I watched television that night thinking about Gay and the knife while stirring the melting contents of my ice cream bowl into a mush. The next morning, furry bundle under one arm and shiny new trap slung over the opposite shoulder, I followed Gay. The sideknife sheath bounced on her curved right hip as she climbed the vestibule stairs. I took a greasy sack of hamburgers and french fries from Mom, waved to the Ihlys and scooted up the stairs of the waiting train. Once inside, I threw the beaver pelt up onto an overhead rack and looking over at Gay, slumped back into my seat for the long ride home.

CHAPTER 12
Changing of the Guard

As snow melted from the roots of trees in the forest and increasing sunlight warmed late April air in our valley, I hung my new #3 trap up in the chalet with the other traps, its promise still unfulfilled. My attention had turned to the things we'd not done since the previous fall. First on the list was swimming.

I stood on the shore of the second slough straight across the field from our cabin that morning and watched the silty gray overflow waters of the Susitna River pass by. The current traveled at a four mile an hour clip. On the far shore of the slough, up to his knees in water, John stood on the swamped bank of Cottonwood Island waiting for my signal. I looked upstream, waited for a small ice cake to pass by, then dropped my arm. John dove into the water on the opposite shore, covering the twenty feet of temporary river channel in a few seconds. Then, clawing his way up on shore next to me, he stood dripping and chattering.

"It's my turn now. You watch." I moved up to the shore's edge, took a quick look upstream and plunged in.

The current grabbed and carried me while I tried to swim the distance quickly. Once at the opposite shore, I worked my way back upstream in the knee deep water. When John's arm dropped, I made the return trip.

We both took several more turns. Then with numb fingers, we pulled our clothes back on. I couldn't button my shirt so I tied the tails in a knot about my waist and headed home behind my brother. The field was free of snow earlier than anywhere else in the valley because the river jam in February left behind a dusting of silt over the water saturated snow. The silt had absorbed heat from an early spring sun, and now our field had turned into one big mud hole.

By looking at the number of river snags that the flood had left behind, I knew there was more field work to be done that summer, but as Dad had said, we all should have been grateful that the five feet of snow cover kept the flood waters from whisking our topsoil away.

Suddenly chilled now, I ran through a small patch of ankle deep snow that was shaded in the alders near our spring and leapt across our water hole. John, who wore his boots, which he hadn't taken the time to lace up, was still negotiating the rocks at our spring crossing by the time I arrived at the cabin.

"Where have you two been?" Gay busily swept the one room. "You know Mom's coming home today. I need help cleaning up around here."

"We've got plenty of time. The train isn't due for another two hours yet." I wiped the bottoms of my muddied feet on the door sill.

"Don't do that there." Gay came over to me. "I just told you I was trying to clean this place."

"It's only a little mud. It'll dry and fall off."

"I don't care. I said don't do it." She brushed the dirt away using brisk strokes with the broom. "And comb your hair, will you? You've got sticks in it."

"I'm waiting for it to dry first." I retreated outside, picking my boots up off the porch as I went.

I walked over to where Spook was tied. He lay on his side taking in a late morning sun bath and let out little satisfied moans when I sat on his house and rubbed my wet, cold feet in this thick fur. Then, feet dry and clean, I put on my socks and boots.

John entered the cabin while I sat, then came out again with a full slop pail and water buckets. "You get the water and I'll empty the garbage." He put the buckets down in front of me.

I picked them up.

"Then Gay says we need wood."

"Okay. Okay." I started down the water trail again.

In an hour we had the cabin cleaned and stocked to Gay's satisfaction. Then she sent us out to call Dad for lunch. Dad had been trying to find fifty spruce trees he'd chopped down early the previous winter as a start on our new house. At last count he'd come across thirty-five of them. We followed the forest trail and before long saw Dad in the woods. The crusted snow gave way under his feet and he sank past his knees with each step towards us and the packed trail.

John jumped off the trail and ran to him, making several circles around Dad as he struggled. "Having problems, Pop?"

Dad looked up and John did a little jig on the hard white surface.

"Your time is coming," Dad said and heaved his body forward.

"Gay says it's time to come in for lunch, then meet the train," I said when Dad reached the trail.

"I was heading home anyway. I found all the trees and as soon as this snow goes, we can start hauling them in."

"Are we going to build this year, then?" John still danced on the crusted snow beside the trail.

"I guess that depends on whether or not I go to work."

Mom had written Dad about the possibility of his going to work for her boss. He had a construction business and did jobs all over the state. Mom said Dad might have a chance to work on one of those jobs.

Gay hurried us through lunch, then Dad made me help her with the dishes. Before heading for the section house, I combed my hair but didn't put a bow in it like Gay had with hers. When Mom got off I helped carry the boxes home, then ate a piece of watermelon while she told Dad about a job.

"But there's work to be done here, Alice. I don't know if I should leave this early. We have the field to clean out, house logs to bring in. This is the year we planned to build the house."

"If you don't go now there might not be another opening for a long time. The kids and I can handle anything that needs to be done."

"But Adak is so far away. It's out on the Aleutian Chain. I won't be able to get home for visits like you did. That's fifteen hundred miles away."

I thought about that. Actually, things had been running pretty smoothly with Mom's absence. But then, things had been pretty peaceful all around since Sandra had left. I enjoyed Mom's visits home. It was wonderful to share with her the things I'd learned both in school and about the homestead. The few times she had come home it was like a big party. But then, after a couple of days, I felt anxious to get back to my routine of studying and playing. I had the feeling that somehow I wouldn't be doing things like swimming with the ice cakes at the second slough if she knew about it. Not that Dad really allowed us to do things like that. He just didn't keep track of what we were getting in to as much Mom would have.

"Well." I tuned back into the conversation and saw Mom shrug her shoulders. "That's all he has open. And I doubt if there will be a job any closer later on. My boss does most of his work on the Aleutians."

Dad stirred his coffee. "I guess we don't have much choice then. Are you sure you and the kids can manage all right all summer, maybe all winter, long?"

"I'll tell you one thing. There will be more school work done while I'm home than there was this past winter." Mom looked at John. "I opened our mail on my train ride home. The University of Nebraska says you're still on the first half of ninth grade English and that if you don't finish by June they'll have to charge us to extend the course another year."

"I don't have time to do that dumb stuff." John looked down.

"Now that I'm here you will. Either that or go to school in town. There's no excuse for being that far behind in your schoolwork. Nor you either." Mom switched her accusing look toward Gay and me.

"University of Nebraska courses are harder than Calvert Courses," John began.

"Don't give me that. If you had been given proper supervision this past winter you would have kept up."

"Alice, you can lead a horse to water but you can't make him drink," Dad said. "I figure if the kids really want to finish school they'll do their work without constant prodding."

"It's the job of the supervisor to see that the lessons get done on schedule," Mom continued. "At least John was up with his studies when I left. Now he's going to have to work all summer at his courses. He won't even be ready for the tenth grade by this fall."

"That's because I refuse to do his school work for him like you did last year. If you want to do it again, that's fine. But I'm not going to."

"I won't do it for him either. But it will get done, even if we have to postpone all the summer work."

"Well, we'll at least be postponing building the house again this year," Dad said. "I just wish I had time to do that before leaving."

Mom shook her head. "My boss wants you to report for work in two weeks."

"That gives us enough time to drag the junk out of the field anyway," Dad said. "We'll start on it tomorrow and with any time left we can haul the logs into a pile near the house. Maybe this summer the kids can peel them so they are all ready to make the house with next summer."

"Yeah. Maybe we could start building without Dad to give him a head start next spring," said John, chewing his piece of melon rapidly.

"Beginning right now, you're not doing anything but schoolwork. That goes for Gay too. Melody can help. She's the only one who has kept halfway on schedule."

I avoided her praising eyes. I had done a little sneak peeking on exams the previous winter, and now wondered whether or not Gay and John had taken the same liberties.

CHAPTER 13
Mr. Check-um-Everything

Mom stuck to her word, restricting John and Gay to the cabin the next few weeks while I worked with my parents. We had done the field work and began hauling logs within our limited time schedule. The snow disappeared rapidly now and on the last day Dad was home we made one final scouting trip out to the woods to spot the few remaining trees. When we returned for the Cat, John had his head under the cowling.

"What are you doing?" Dad filled the Cat with gas while John still poked around.

"My farm machinery course says to come out here and find the rocker arm on the tractor." He held up the text and pointed to a black and white picture. "It's supposed to look like this."

"What does it do?" Dad asked.

"I don't know. That's the question I'm supposed to answer."

"Let's see." Dad took the text book, orienting the picture several different ways.

"Beats me." He handed it back.

"What am I supposed to write then?" John asked.

"Make a guess at it," Dad suggested.

"What's the problem?" Mom came from the cabin where she'd gone for some bug repellent.

"John can't find the rocker arm," I said.

"What's that?"

"If I knew I wouldn't be out here looking for it."

"Don't get smart with me young man."

"I'm not getting smart. If I were smart I'd know what a rocker arm was. How do they expect me to find something from a picture? It's not even a picture of a Cat like ours."

"Let me see." Mom took the book and John waited nearby.

"Do you know, Leon?" She looked up a few minutes later.

Dad shook his head.

"Why don't you just write your instructor and ask for more information. Tell him you don't understand the picture."

81

John took the book back. "I'm not going to ask him anything. Every time I send a lesson in he sends it back with red check marks all over it. My lessons look like they've bled to death. He says he can't read my writing." John slammed the text closed. "He should talk. It took me two days to figure out what he wrote the last time. I can't even tell what his name is, he signs it so funny."

Mom and Dad looked at each other. Then Mom followed my brother who headed back for the cabin.

"Well, the only way you're going to get through these problems is by writing to someone who knows about them and can help you," I heard her say before going inside.

Dad finished filling the Cat and pulled the funnel from its gas tank.

"I think we'll just go ahead without Mom. She's going to be busy for a little while." He stepped toward the seat, pausing. "Do you want to learn how to drive this thing?"

"Sure!"

"Okay, hop up here then. Someone is going to have to know how to run this contraption while I'm gone."

I hopped up into the seat. Dad stood on the trailer hitch behind the seat and held onto its back. He talked me through starting and gearing the Cat. Then I set the throttle, put the piece of machinery in gear and released the clutch. We started off in a slow crawl and under Dad's instructions I worked the two levers in front of me. The left one made us go left, the right one, right. After a few close calls with nearby spruce trees, I caught on, shifted to the next highest gear and headed down the logging road with Dad hanging on behind.

Dad let me back the Cat up to the logs we were going to haul in. Then he cinched them together with the choker. When he gave the go ahead signal I slowly released the clutch. The choker bit into the logs and we headed back down the trail. Actually, John already knew how to operate the Cat, a fact he'd been lording over me for quite some time. I cracked a big smile when we met Mom walking the road towards us and stopped the crawler tractor for a few seconds while she walked off to the side.

"Back so soon?" Dad shouted, smiling.

"I just sat down and explained to him what he had to do. All the children need is a firm hand."

We made several more trips and by the time all the logs were dragged into place in a large pile behind the cabin, I'd become pretty handy with maneuvering the Cat. Better yet, I'd seen John watching my comings and goings out of the back cabin window. Now Dad motioned with his index finger across his throat and I pushed the 'kill' button on the engine.

"I've got to quit and get cleaned up." Dad came over to me. "If you want you can take the pry bar and push these last logs into place with the others. Then when you get the chance, start peeling them."

I looked at the pile of logs in front of me. They were stacked high over my head. They didn't look much like a reward for finishing my lessons on time.

"I'll help you." Mom picked up a bar. The two of us added the last logs to the pile.

When we got inside, John was busy with his school lesson.

"If you're going to get that letter to your teacher on the train with Dad you'd better start writing," Mom suggested.

"I already started, but I need help." John pulled a paper out of his notebook.

"Well, let's see what you've got." Mom took the paper and put on her reading glasses. "You can't send this!"

"Why not? It'd serve him right."

"Just put his correct name on it." She handed him the paper.

"I can't read his correct name." John took the paper and crumpled it.

"Let me see his letter to you," Mom sighed.

My brother gave his last corrected lesson to her and she turned the piece of paper around in her hand much like Dad had done with the textbook earlier. "It looks like Hanson," she decided.

"I think my name fits him better." John ripped another sheet of paper from his notebook.

"What did you call him?" I came closer.

John picked up the crumpled piece of paper and cleared his throat. "Dear Mr. Check–um–Everything," he began.

Dad, who had been standing near the stove with a fresh cup of coffee, choked on a mouthful. John smiled broadly.

"Leon!" Mom chastised. "You shouldn't encourage that sort of thing. It's no wonder these children haven't gotten their schoolwork done. It looks like I came home just in time."

CHAPTER 14
Nick Botner

With our little Shetland sheep dog, Ren, beside me and several spruce grouse hanging from my belt, I followed the ridge path above the first slough on my way home. The field below me had finally begun producing the lush growth we all had waited for, but not until Mom, John and I had reseeded the entire flooded area. I stopped now, sat down and leaned my back against a birch tree. Dad would have been proud to see the green field. But he was on Adak Island, and the chances of us walking through the field, tall grass tugging at our ankles as he took head samples from the various types of grass, were few. If we were lucky, he'd make it home for a Christmas visit.

Ren nuzzled me, begging to continue the hunt. I sat stroking his head and continued looking at the field. So far that year, Ren and I had kept each other company most of the time. Gay and John were still struggling over school lessons and had been restricted to the cabin.

Ren pawed me anxiously.

"Okay, boy." I got up, following behind him on the ridge trail. We were almost home when the little dog's tail started spinning.

"No more, Ren," I commanded. "Let's go home."

He looked at me, cocked his head slightly, then nose out straight and tail twirling madly, streaked out into the forest. I soon lost sight of his sable fur in the thick woods.

"Dumb dog." I shifted my .22 and kept walking the trail home.

"You're back early." Mom looked up from something she stirred on the stove. "No luck?"

"Plenty of luck." I'd left the hens outside.

"Where's Ren?" John looked up from a book.

"He ran off after more hens. I let him go."

"I'll go after him." John got up.

"No you won't," Mom warned.

"I've been studying all day." John slumped into his chair.

"You can go meet the train today, but that's all."

I left as John again opened his textbook. When the hens were dressed I brought them back inside. It seemed if the birds were skinned and soaked in a mild salt water solution some of the strong flavor in the meat was lost.

"How can I study around here if Melody is going to make all that racket?" John slammed his text closed.

"Melody, would you mind being a little less noisy? Your brother and sister are trying to study."

"I was just preparing the grouse."

"Do it quietly then."

I did, then went back outside. Most of the wood in the shed had already been chopped during the past few months. But there were some gnarled blocks left that I now tackled with a sledge hammer and wedge. I'd just finished splitting the first one in half when Mom came out to the shed.

"Do you have to do that now? It makes a terrible racket in the house."

"Oh." I put the sledge hammer down. "How about if I carry some water and fill up the extra storage cans?"

"You filled everything up this morning, even the carrying buckets are full." Mom paused. "Why don't you go for a walk?"

"I've already been out hunting all morning."

"Well. Then go up to Botner's place and see if everything is all right."

I hesitated. "Can I take Spook?"

"Sure. Just don't make any noise."

I slipped the harness over Spook's head and fastened the chest strap. Then, leading him back to a bicycle we'd found in Botner's basement, I hooked him to the frame with the end of the traces.

"Let's go, boy," I commanded a few minutes later.

Spook began a dignified trot up to the section house trail with the bicycle in tow.

Botner's house was quiet and lonely. I spent enough time to check that everything was okay, then hurried Spook to the section house to meet the train. I had hoped for a letter from Dad, but all that came were graded school lessons for Gay and John. The other daily routine came that evening when we listened to Northwind on the radio. Nick Botner at Stephan Lake got a message that somebody was coming in the next day by float plane. There were messages for people in

Talkeetna and Wasilla, two towns south of us. I lost interest after the first half of the program and almost missed the next message.

"To Alice and the kids at Gold Creek."

I looked up.

"Nick and I will be on the train tomorrow. We're bringing Leon home to celebrate the Fourth of July. Love, Madge."

"Dad!" I jumped up. "Mom, Dad's coming home."

She let a smile go. "Yes. I didn't want to let you kids get your hopes up because Leon didn't know whether or not he could get the time off and catch a cargo plane in from Adak."

Even with Dad's impending arrival, Mom didn't let up on Gay and John. In fact, I left the cabin early in the morning that next day at Mom's request, so they could have maximum quiet and get their week's lessons out ahead of time. That way they wouldn't have to study while Dad was home.

I again found myself up on the ridge, watching the field and petting Ren. I hadn't been there long when a plane on floats made several low passes over our slough then circled, appearing to have landed somewhere on the river near the bridge. I waited fifteen minutes for the plane to leave. Then when it didn't, ran down the ridgeside to the cabin.

"So?" John looked up when I told the news. "I saw a plane land there last week."

"What for?"

"They were from the Coast and Geodetic Survey out of Anchorage. They're rigging a bosun's chair across the river so they can read the level of the water and take samples."

"How do you know?" I asked.

"I went over there when it landed."

"When?" Mom wanted to know.

"When you asked me to go check Botner's and Ihlys' houses for roof leaks."

"You were to look at those houses and come right home."

"It only took a little longer to go down to the plane."

A knock on the cabin door diverted Mom's attention. Still giving John a stern look, she opened it.

A tall, clean-shaven, husky man with a ruddy complexion filled the doorway. Another smaller man stood behind him.

"Hi. I'm Nick Botner." He extended his right hand. "We saw smoke coming from the cabin and thought we'd stop in for a visit."

Mom shook the offered hand. "Come on in. We heard your message last night. I thought you were at Stephan Lake."

"We were." Botner took his hunter's cap off.

"You're the ones in the plane that landed at the bridge, right?" I asked.

"That's right. I'm having a box car let off at the siding here at Gold Creek tonight when the local freight comes through. It's full of building supplies for my lodge at the lake. We're going to transport them by float plane up there. The river is rough for docking and loading, though, so I thought we'd ask your permission to dock in your slough."

"Well, I don't know." Mom hesitated.

"We won't be hurting anything. The salmon aren't in yet so they won't be disturbed." Botner continued. "And it sure would help us out."

"Yes," Mom answered. "I guess that would be all right."

"If you'd feel better about it, we could wait until Leon gets in today and ask him. We heard your message last night, too."

"No. I'm certain it's okay. Leon wouldn't mind." Mom smiled now. "Would you fellows like a cup of coffee?"

Nick told us about his lodge on Stephan Lake and his daughter, Nikki, who was up there waiting for them to come in that day. After several hours of talking with him about the country, wildlife and fishing, he made the suggestion that one of us children go back with them to spend the night.

"We'll be loading things out of here for a couple of days. I could take one of the kids back with me this trip and bring them home on a shuttle trip tomorrow."

"The children have school work to catch up on." Mom looked at me. "Except for Melody."

"Well, how about it?" Botner's smile was infectious.

"I don't know. Dad's coming home today. I'd like to be here to meet him."

"He'll be here for a few days." Mom handed me a comb for my

hair. "You'll get to see him. But you might never get another chance to see Stephan Lake."

I took the comb, running it through my long straight hair.

"You're just the right size for the jump seat," Botner encouraged.

"I'll go." I put the comb down.

"Then let's get moving." Botner opened the door.

I followed the two men up to the section house road and down the tracks to the bridge. They had docked the plane parallel to the shoreline, tying it by the front and back of one of the floats. It rocked to and fro as passing current worked by.

"I'll help you get in first." Botner jumped onto the tied float. He opened the flimsy door of the plane and leaned the front seat forward. With him holding onto my arm, I crawled up into the back of the small plane, and sat on the plywood board seat.

"Don't forget to fasten your seat belt." He put the front seat back into position. The pilot crawled over to the left side while Botner remained out on the float, untying the docking rope.

I tied a rope belt over my lap and looked out the small window to my left. When the engine started, my mouth felt dry. I'd never flown before, not even in one of those big planes like Dad did when he went to Adak.

"You ready?" Botner yelled over the noise of the airplane.

The pilot nodded.

Botner hopped into the right hand seat in front of me, closing the door behind him. Suddenly I realized that on his way in he had pushed us off from the shore and now the plane headed downstream…backwards.

CHAPTER 15
Stephan Lake

Botner busily strapped himself in with his own seat belt while we continued, tail first, down the river. I could see the Susitna River Bridge which we'd been almost docked underneath getting smaller as mid–river current carried the little plane away. Then the pilot looked at Botner, back at me, and added power.

The plane shuddered slightly in the water, then began holding its own against the powerful current. I felt slight relief with the fact that we were headed forwards as the rough current we now fought began bouncing us inside the plane. The bridge ahead grew larger. I looked down at the left float. It skied over the river surface but we still weren't airborne. Just before reaching the bridge, the plane popped off the water and our pilot flew it under the bridge, gaining altitude as soon as we cleared the metal structure. We made one low pass over our cabin doing a wing–wag, then began going into climbing circles until high enough to get over Disappointment mountain.

"You all right?" Botner yelled back to me.

I grinned now, nodding. Botner turned to face frontward again. The trip would take about twenty minutes. I looked for caribou on the miles of tundra–covered mountainscape below, but didn't see any. It was pretty early for caribou in this area though. They'd have to migrate in. The noise of the plane made it impossible to talk, so I just kept watch outside my window until Botner finally turned again, pointing ahead. I followed his directions to see a large area where the tundra dipped into a forest–filled basin. As we approached I saw a long lake.

Minutes later the pilot throttled back, making a straight in approach. Our touch–down was smoother than take–off, floats sending great arcs of water off their trailing edges while ducks and geese flew up in small flocks on either side of us. We taxied up to a nearby wooden pier where a girl in shorts waited.

I was the last out of the plane and Nikki greeted me. She was small, but looked older than Gay.

"Melody came up to do some fishing." Botner tied the plane off.

"Why don't you fix her up with some gear and the two of you can go out in the boat after we refuel the plane and take off again."

"Sure." Nikki turned to me. "C'mon. I'll show you the lodge."

"Do you go to school by correspondence up here?" I looked around me. I had thought Gold Creek was remote, but this area was in total wilderness. At least our homestead was reachable by railroad.

"Until I can figure a way out of it."

"I'll bet you just love it up here. Just you and your Dad with all the fishing and hunting."

"And no boys," Nikki added in a flat tone.

"Your father said that in the winter time the caribou come across the frozen lake in such large herds that you don't even have to aim to get one. You just point your rifle in the general direction and fire."

We had reached the lodge now and Nikki pushed the door open. Botner had told us it was twenty feet wide and one hundred feet long. It was made exclusively from spruce logs cut from the little basin valley that surrounded them. The logs were huge and varnished until they glistened, just like the ones that made up the house at Gold Creek which now belonged to Dr. Maddock. Picnic–type dining room tables lined the front wall where we entered. Large plate glass windows in front of them gave a magnificent view of the lake.

"This is just beautiful." I sat down.

Nikki went into a kitchen bar area across from me, punching down a large vat of raised bread dough. "Yeah. Well when you have to look at it all the time as well as cook for the hunters and fishermen, it tends to get to you after awhile."

I watched her a moment, then glanced across the lake, seeing another small cabin. "Who lives over there?" I pointed.

She came over, picked up a nearby pair of binoculars and stood looking for a moment. "Some guys out vacationing. They just flew in a little while ago. There's a real cute one with them."

"Oh." I accepted the binoculars Nikki extended. "Do you do any trapping?"

"No. But Daddy does." She went back to her bread.

In a short while we were again at the lake and waited for the men to leave.

"The boat is almost out of gas," Botner warned. "We're bringing some back this next trip, but until then don't take it out any farther than you're willing to row back."

"I won't, Daddy." Nikki pecked him on the cheek.

We watched the plane take off, then Nikki hopped into the boat. "Ready?"

"Sure." I hesitated. "Aren't we going to need some fishing poles though?"

"Good idea." She jumped out of the boat and I followed her back up to the lodge.

"Hurry up. They'll be back soon," She prodded.

I selected several different lures for my pole from a tackle box, then followed her down to the lake. She started the boat as I got in.

"As soon as we get out a little ways you can let some line out and troll."

I did. And no sooner than we'd gotten underway, I felt a strong strike. "I got one," I shouted, reeling in.

Nikki pulled the engine back to an idle. "Hurry up and bring him in. I'll net him for you."

In a few minutes of playing, I landed my prize. The lake trout was over a foot long and the first I'd ever seen. All we had in Gold Creek were grayling and gold–fin dolly varden that never got over pan size. I eagerly returned my line to the water as she revved the engine again and we started underway.

"I got another one," I yelled.

"I don't believe this." Nikki reduced the engine again.

This time I reeled my catch in even faster, netting him myself while Nikki sat, watching.

"Aren't you going to fish?" I hauled the flopping trout into the boat.

"I had planned on fishing a little closer to the far shore." She reached for the throttle.

"Oh. Okay. I won't troll anymore until we get there."

I had a hard time keeping my promise as Nikki poured on the power, boat spewing a rooster tail of water behind us. A few hundred feet from the other cabin, she reduced power again.

"Quick, put your line in the water." She grabbed up her pole making a long professional cast before I'd even set my reel.

I noticed now that a man had come out of the cabin.

"You know him?" I asked as she returned a wave.

"Not yet."

"Is he the cute one?"

"Yeah." She jerked her pole. "I got one."

Nikki began reeling slowly while I watched. "You've got too much slack," I said. "He's going to spit the lure."

"I don't care."

"Let me play him then."

"Are you kidding? That guy is watching us." Nikki reeled in a few more turns. "It just got away anyhow." She reeled her line all the way in then, shrugging her shoulders in a gesture to the young man on the bank. Then she looked down at her wristwatch.

"Oh, sugar! Look at the time. We've got to get back to the lodge or my bread will rise over the bowl!"

Nikki started the engine and we made it halfway across the lake before it sputtered and died.

"Out of gas." She frowned. "I knew we shouldn't have taken so long getting over there."

"I'll row. I don't mind." I worked the oars out of the bottom of the boat. With her help we put them in the oar locks.

She joined me on the bench seat, each of us handling an oar that slapped rhythmically at the water. "This is just beautiful. It's so far away from everything."

"You won't feel that way in a few years."

"Do you really like that guy back there?"

"He's a guy, isn't he?" She laughed.

"I don't know. Something must be wrong with me, I guess."

"Cheer up, kid. You'll make it. I'm just fifteen and look at me."

"You're fifteen?" I stopped rowing.

"Sure. How old did you think I was?"

"Sixteen, at the very least."

Nikki looked pleased. "Well, I just matured early, that's all. You'll catch up."

"But that's the problem. I'm not sure I want to."

"How old are you?"

"Thirteen."

"And you mean to tell me you're not interested in boys yet?"

I shook my head.

"I can't even remember the time when I wasn't interested in boys," Nikki laughed.

When we reached the dock she tied a rope around a pier.

"If you want, you can clean those fish right here on the dock. If you hold some guts under water a fish will come up and take them right out of your hand."

I began cleaning while Nikki ran up to the lodge. I just about had a fish tame enough to take my hand–held offering when the sound of an approaching motor caught my ear. I looked up to see a boat coming from the opposite shore. Nikki was down on the dock with me before the boat and young man operating it coasted up to the pier.

"Saw you had a little trouble with that last fish." He smiled at Nikki. "Did he get away?"

"Not necessarily." Nikki winked at me.

I looked back down at the water, not paying the other two any attention as they continued talking. Then, once again we heard an engine. This time we watched a plane come in for a landing.

"Oh, sugar." Nikki held a hand over her eyes to shade them from the sun. "It's Daddy."

We waited for the plane to taxi in. Again Nick was the first out.

"Did my Dad get off the train?" I asked.

"He sure did. He told me to tell you to catch lots of fish and have a good time."

I did just that, going out with Nick and Nikki that evening to troll the deep waters of Stephan Lake for trout. Then we fished the outlet for huge grayling and rainbow. The next morning, boxful of trout on my lap where I sat in the jumpseat of the plane, I waved goodbye to Nikki as we taxied out onto the lake for take–off.

The trip back seemed to take longer than the one over. I kept looking ahead, thinking I saw us approaching the back crest of our mountains only to have more tundra appear in front of us. Finally the pilot cut power and our little plane glided downward into Gold Creek valley.

After circling the cabin once we bumped to a landing in a river channel directly below the mouth of the first slough. Then the pilot taxied us into the slough where John and Dad stood waiting by one of the banks. Dad caught the rope Nick threw to him and pulled the plane up close to shore.

"Well, how'd she do?" Dad smiled broadly.

"There isn't a fish left in Stephan Lake without a notch in its top fin." Nick shouted while I crawled from the back of the plane with my box of trout.

"Ho–ly mackerel. Look at the size of these things." My brother had ripped open the box and held one up for Dad to admire.

We helped Botner load the plane with supplies and then watched it taxi out of the slough and take–off downstream. John insisted on carrying the box of fish home. Dad and I followed slowly behind.

"You had a good time up there, huh?" He said. "It's pretty nice country, isn't it."

"It's beautiful." I paused while we walked through our tall field grass with its full, ripe heads of timothy and rye. "But you know what? It's not half as good as what we have here."

"Oh?"

"Naw. I like Gold Creek a lot better."

Dad cuffed me playfully on the back of the head. "C'mon. We'd better get back to the cabin before John tells a whopper of a fish story for you."

CHAPTER 16
The Surprise

I followed John down the hillside to the beaver swamp. He took care to brush out the trail down the ridgeside wide enough now so that when the heavy snowfalls came that winter the alders alongside the trail wouldn't be forced into it. Trapping season wasn't going to open for another week, and beaver season not for several months. But we had decided to get a head start on planning our route.

A frozen alder slapped me in the face now, bringing tears. I bent it away, still following John downward. We hoped to use Spook on the trapline that year, but if we didn't start getting snow soon, the sled would be useless. We also wanted to have Spook train a new puppy we had gotten the previous fall. Spook had wandered off for a few days last summer and several months later a neighbor several miles south insisted Spook had sired some pups. They were all black and that seemed to convince Mom, especially after she saw how cute they were. We had called our new puppy "Papeete."

"Be careful," I warned now as John reached the bottom of the hill and stepped out onto a clear sheet of ice. He bent down occasionally to chip away at the frozen surface.

"It's safe," he reported, walking ahead cautiously.

Even though I was just as eager to reach the huge beaver house in the center of the pond, I kept a safe distance behind my brother.

"Look at that feed pile, would you?" John stood on top of the house moments later. "I'll bet there's a whole family of super blankets living in here."

I nodded, looking at the huge pile of stored winter feed stretching out from the house to the edge of the large dam.

"Let's stake it right over there." John pointed, then headed for an area of ice riddled with air pockets. He began chopping a hole in the ice with his hatchet while I unsheathed the machete and went to a nearby alder stand. Several whacks brought the alder down. By the time I'd trimmed and hauled it back to John, he had a hole chopped through the ice. I pushed the pole down through the water and sunk it into the silty bottom.

John took a roll of bright red surveyor's tape from his jacket pocket, broke a long length free and tied it to the tip of the stake. We'd been staking beaver houses most of the week. The whole purpose behind the procedure was to find the best place to make a set before the deep winter snows covered everything.

"What now?" John rolled the tape.

"I think we should put a wolverine set around this house somewhere. Whitey says they can smell live beaver houses."

John looked around, pointing to a large spruce tree off the edge of the pond and almost directly back down the path we'd just made.

"We'll string some bait up on that tree and put the #3 and some #2's under it."

"Okay. That looks good." I motioned with my head. "Let's travel this swamp until it ends and cut straight through the woods. We should pick up the river."

John slipped his hatchet in his belt and this time followed me across the remainder of the swamp. We kept to the lowlands which soon turned from swamp to muskeg hummocks, then forest. Keeping a true course, we traveled only about a mile before breaking through some alders lining the river bank. John pulled out his pocket watch.

"We made good time. Walking this whole line should only take three or four hours."

"This is going to take as much time as the other one then," I said. "We won't have enough daylight to cover both in one day."

"We'll split up then. You can check one. I'll do the other."

"Okay. But we rotate. I'm not going to get stuck with that hill everyday." I looked back the direction we had just come.

"But whoever gets this run, gets Spook too," John added quickly.

I agreed and we started across the frozen river towards home.

By the time Dad came home for Christmas, we hoped to have all the stretching boards full of furs for him to admire. Dad hadn't been able to get home since the Fourth of July trip and as I walked behind John now I thought about where the summer went.

As Mom promised, my school books had arrived in August. Of the four courses required for the ninth grade, English, Algebra and General Science were mandatory. I only had one elective course and selected General Agriculture. I liked my agriculture and English course and worked on them most of the time. But science and algebra gave me problems so, like Gay and John, I was slowly slipping behind in my studies. I figured, though, that I could study through the next summer if I had to. Right then the trapline seemed more important.

When we got home, Mom looked up from a letter. "Leon says there's going to be something coming up on the freight tonight. You two keep your ears open for the train. We want to be up there to help unload."

"What's Dad sending?"

"He says it's a surprise."

That night when we heard the freight coming, John and I ran ahead of Mom and Gay and stood waiting. By the time Mom and Gay caught up with us, the freight train was already pulling slowly past the section house. Local freight was always let off at the rear of the train and we waited impatiently while the crewmen near the engine released it plus a box car, then worked the switch so the engine could off load the car on the side.

"Are they ever going to finish up there?" Gay looked to the north switch, kicking her feet together.

I looked from the engine at the north switch back to the caboose which had barely cleared the south bend a mile away. Then the engineer finally tooted the horn. A high-ball signal was given by lantern light from the front of the train and confirmed by the rear. The cars began to slowly move past us, picking up speed.

"It's not going to stop," John shouted as the cars began whisking past. I watched the caboose come near, then pass us. We stood looking after the red light as it disappeared around the bend.

"I guess we'd better meet it on the way back tomorrow and pray Dad didn't send anything that will spoil." Mom turned.

We followed her down the boardwalk.

The noise of the section house screen door made me look up. The section foreman held it half open and stood with his parka on. "You want to open that car now?" he said.

"What car?" Mom said.

"That one." He nodded to the box car left on the siding.

"That's ours?"

THE SURPRISE

He looked at a manifest. "Says here. 'Erickson – one box car at Gold Creek'." He lowered the paper. "You want in there now or not?"

"Sure." Mom looked at the car.

The man picked up a tool to cut the seal on the car doors then walked across the tracks with us right behind. The car had been left off in the shadows. John held a flashlight beam on the seal as the man worked. He pulled the freed door release lever up and left without a word. Gay and I helped John slide the large door back. Then John hoisted himself up into the car and Gay handed him the flashlight. The beam flickered off the walls for a moment, then settled somewhere past my limited vision in an area at the far end of the wood–lined walls.

"Would you look at that!" John's voice echoed.

I climbed in after Gay and we helped Mom. John still held the beam steady and we followed him to the pile of boxes and sacks in front of us.

"This can't be ours." Mom walked around a portion of the mound. The flashlight beam landed on an inventory sheet taped to one of the first boxes and Gay picked it up.

"It says Erickson." She flipped through pages that rustled loudly. John held the light on it. The car was cold. I made little smoke rings with my breath and watched as they caught in the flashlight's beam, then drifted from view.

On the last page I recognized several lines of Dad's unique scribble.

" 'I want to see some meat on those bones when I come home for Christmas'." Gay tilted the page towards the light.

I looked down at a box near me now, picking it up to read the label. "It's a case of marshmallows!" I said.

John flashed the light to other boxes, reading aloud. "Canned kernel corn, canned whole chicken, that one over there says Devils food cake mix."

"It's all on the list." Gay flipped from page to page trying to keep up with John's recitation.

"It's a case order." Mom, quiet until now, took the list from Gay. "That's how they order things for camps. I'll bet Dad got a good deal though his camp wholesaler. We'd better get an organized inventory started. Two of you go back for the Cat and stoneboat."

Both John and I jumped from the car, leaving Mom and Gay to go over the list. Hooking the Cat to the stoneboat, John put the machine into third gear and headed it back up the trail at its fastest clip while I stood on the stoneboat that dragged behind.

Mom and Gay had already moved some boxes near the box car door, checking items off the inventory as they did so. We made five full trips with the Cat, carrying away our booty while Mom checked and double checked the inventory aloud. There were 100 pound bags of flour, both rye and white. The same held true for sugar: brown, white and powdered. We called off cases of cereal, hot and cold, canned vegetables, fruit, meat, coffee and cocoa.

By late that night we'd finally managed to store the boxes in the chalet and bags of sugar up in the front half of the loft which had been empty since Sandra's departure. Then, tired and somewhat giddy, I sat in the cabin drinking coffee while going over the inventory.

Up until that time all our grocery orders had consisted of staple items. But that night I discovered we had case after case of cake, pie and ice cream mixes. Candy, peanut butter, store bought jellies, canned bacon, different specialty breads, even relishes and other condiments that I could barely remember were included in the order.

There were several items that Dad had neglected to order though. The little boxes on the inventory beside items such as corned beef and Spam remained vacant.

CHAPTER 17
Death

By the time trapping season opened, both John and I had had our fill of delicacies and were ready to have a surprise of our own when Dad came home at Christmas time. We'd found out he had been laid off and would be home for good, or at least until the following spring. But our first few weeks of trapping were anything but success-ful and by the day Dad and the Ihlys got off the train, we had little to show for our efforts. We had enough snow to use the dog sled on the swamp run, but it was still too difficult a trail for Papeete. So the day after Dad came home John headed out with only Spook. I knew he'd be able to cover his line faster than I could mine so was surprised when I got back home and John hadn't returned yet. When he did, though, he was sitting on top of our first wolverine.

"I knew I should have taken the swamp run today." I looked on with the others as John dumped his load.

"You should be glad you didn't. This thing was alive and frothing at the mouth when I came up to him. The #3 trap was the only one holding him." John raised a hind paw. "By one toe."

"I knew it would hold him," I said.

"It's a good thing you didn't go on that run today, Melody," Mom added. "You probably couldn't have handled this animal."

"I could've done it."

"He went right to the top of that beaver house before coming over to the set," John continued.

"Whitey said he'd do that."

"I don't want to hear about it." Gay went inside.

"You would have felt different if it was your throat he'd been try-ing for." John followed her.

"I'm not listening." She put her hands over her ears and started to hum a tune.

The following day was clear and cold. I sat by the wolverine hide wiping it down and removing pieces of fat and flesh we'd missed by lantern light the previous night. Gay strapped a huge turkey, roaster pan and all, onto a pack board for the trip to the Ihlys' house. They'd come up to spend Christmas with us in Gold Creek and we were supplying the turkey for Mrs. Ihly to cook.

"Now don't stay over there too long," Mom said as Gay put the load on her back and slipped into a pair of snowshoes. "I don't want you kids making pests of yourselves."

"I won't." Gay snowshoed up the trail.

My sister kept her promise, returning to the cabin before dinner time.

"How's Madge?"

"Okay." Gay took off the empty pack board. "But I think maybe Mr. Ihly is mad at her, or me."

"What makes you think that?"

"When I was coming up the road to their place, I heard Mr. Ihly chainsawing some wood. Then the saw stopped and when I got to where he'd just felled a tree, he was just sitting there along side it. I said 'hi' to him but he just looked at me. So I went up to their house with the turkey."

"Leon. Do you think we should go up there and see if everything is all right?" Mom asked.

"Naw. He probably thought Gay heard him cursing that chain saw of his and felt embarrassed." Dad looked at the hide I'd just finished final fleshing.

"That's what Mrs. Ihly said when I told her about it. She said Nick really wanted to get those dead trees cut down this time before they fell across the road in a windstorm."

"That explains it then." Mom nodded.

"I still didn't feel right about it. After I told Mrs. Ihly what happened, she didn't call him for lunch. She said he'd come in when he'd cooled down enough. I came home a different way in case he was still mad."

"I wouldn't worry about it," Dad said. "Maybe Mom and I will go see them tomorrow. Nick will probably be laughing about the whole thing then."

We reserved the rest of the afternoon for the weekend radio shows. It was dark when we heard approaching helicopters coming past loud and low.

John left the cabin first, the rest of us after him. Several huge, noisy 'copters circled our area several times. A search light flashed back and forth over the ground up near the section house.

"Maybe they're in trouble," Dad shouted. "Go get a lamp to signal them with."

I ran back inside, grabbing up the lighted Coleman lantern, but by the time I got back outside one of the helicopters had landed. The other hovered in the sky.

"Mr. Ihly!" Gay yelled. "Something's happened to Mr. Ihly! I just know it!"

"Let's not jump to conclusions." Dad took the lantern from me, giving it to John. "You two run up there and see what's happening."

Mom hurried me back into the cabin while Dad stayed outside watching. In a few minutes I heard the helicopters leave.

"It was Mr. Ihly." Gay came in crying. "The section foreman said he had a stroke this afternoon while he was out cutting wood."

"Are you sure?"

"Yes." She sobbed uncontrollably. "I should have known something was wrong."

"Don't blame yourself." Dad held her. "You couldn't have known. Even we didn't think there was anything to get alarmed about."

"But why didn't he say something, anything?" Gay wiped her nose with a tissue Mom gave her.

"It's possible that if he had a stroke just before you got there, he couldn't talk. Or maybe he didn't want to frighten you."

"But he was conscious. When Mrs. Ihly found him he wasn't. If I had only gone past him on my way home."

"We'll just have to wait. It's entirely possible he'll be okay."

"No, he won't." Gay still sobbed. "I know he won't, and it's my fault."

"No, it isn't." Dad cradled her. "Don't ever think that."

The next night I sat, legs dangling over the edge of my top bunk as Dad tuned the radio in for Northwind. Our radio batteries were weak, and the reception poor, but when the announcer began our message, his words came out too clearly.

Dad turned the radio off without saying a word. And later that night I lay on my bunk looking at the cardboard insulated ceiling, listening for a long time to Gay's smothered sobs.

103

CHAPTER 18
Building Bridges

I was happy to see the spring of 1964 come, even though it meant the end of trapping season. Dad had presented me with a beautiful fly fishing rod, reel, line and an assortment of artificial flies for my fourteenth birthday. But, since my birthday fell in November, the new equipment couldn't be tested for another six months. Now that it was July, I made daily trips to the Big Susitna River to practice my fly–casting technique.

With those thoughts, I let Spook dash ahead of me as I walked barefoot on one of the rails towards the bridge. Normally I would have taken the bicycle through the field road. But the bike had just recently fallen into two pieces while John peddled it up to the section house. So now I walked everywhere with Spook, and that morning, almost exactly a year since my fishing trip at Stephan Lake, I passed the north end of a string of gray railroad gang cars parked on the Gold Creek siding.

The bridge and building crew had been at Gold Creek for several weeks. Since their arrival they had been busily swarming around the huge concrete supports of the Big Susitna River Bridge, making frames to pour new concrete and strengthen it. It seemed that the Good Friday earthquake in Anchorage and Southern Alaska that year had taken its toll even as far north as Gold Creek.

Spook swerved in front of me, making me lose my balance on the rail momentarily. Both John and I had been taking turns walking down to the bridge and back both morning and night since breakup time. In those few months, I'd become an expert rail walker. But we weren't doing the daily walk for the fun of it. That spring John had gone down to meet another plane from the Coast and Geodetic Survey in Anchorage. He found some men attaching a small metal box to the ties off the middle portion of the bridge. As it turned out, the gauge they installed needed constant monitoring and both John and I had been hired to measure and record the daily water level. The pay for our service came to a flat twenty dollars a month. We were saving it to buy traps.

When I reached the bridge that morning Spook headed down the embankment to the bridge's base via some old plank stairs. Still walking the rail, I started across the bridge. Walking the rail here required more concentration and the occasional noise of jackhammers below didn't help. I lost balance twice before reaching the small metal box. When I returned I called Spook. And when he didn't come, I started down the old plank stairs. Some of the bridge crew were busy nailing a framework to one of the concrete supports, others stood, waiting. Spook sat next to them, tail sweeping the dirt in a large semicircle on the ground when he saw me approaching.

"This your dog?" a young man with a baby face and dimpled chin asked.

"Yeah. He's my lead dog."

"Lord, he nearly scared us to death. We turned around and saw this huge black dog with white eyes barrelling towards us and thought our number had been called."

"He's friendly," I nodded.

"We know that now." Another man, hard hat on like the first one, kneeled down to pat Spook. "What's your dog's name?"

"Spook."

"Well, Spook is welcome to come down and visit any time." He looked up at me with glimmering hazel eyes. "So are you."

"I'll try to keep him home." I looked away. "I know you've got a lot of work to do around here." I patted my thigh and Spook jumped up, coming over to my side.

"I know all about those guys," John said when I handed Mom a letter from Dad that I'd picked up in our mail box on my way past the section house on my way home. "The one with the dimple is Dave. And that other fellow is Bob."

"You mean the bridge crew guys?" Gay came inside.

"How do you know about them?" I asked.

"I've talked to both of them at the section house while waiting for the passenger trains. They're coming down to go swimming with us this afternoon."

I sat down at the table then and brought my books from the shelf with me. My tenth grade courses had arrived. At least three of them had. I was only allowed to take four courses at a time. So as long as I had my ninth grade General Science to finish I couldn't order my tenth grade elective. I'd already decided my elective would be typing. Dad had a large standard Underwood typewriter he used in college which I could learn on. All I had to do was finish my second semester of General Science and I could order the course.

But even knowing that, I put my General Science text to the side and decided which of my tenth grade courses to begin work on. Biology won out and I opened the text. I continued studying when Gay started getting ready to go swimming.

"Aren't you coming?" She wanted to know.

"I don't have a swimming suit. How can I go swimming with them around?"

"Just wear your cutoffs and a short sleeved shirt," Gay said.

"I don't want to go swimming in a pair of jeans and a shirt. I'll look dumb."

"You won't look dumb." Gay wiggled into her one piece black suit.

"Well, I'm still not going." I closed my textbook and went outside. When I got back Gay and John weren't anywhere around.

"Gay says for you to bring the fellows down to the second slough when they come." Mom looked up from Dad's letter.

"But I'm not going swimming."

"You can still show them where the second slough is."

I sat down at the table. Mom looked up from Dad's letter.

"Is something wrong?"

"No," I mumbled.

"Well, maybe this will make you feel better. Dad is coming home after all. Tomorrow."

"Dad?" I looked up. "Did he get laid off again?"

"I don't know."

"If he comes home we can build the house, can't we?"

"Well, we can at least start." Mom folded the piece of paper.

"Hello. Anybody home?" I recognized Dave's voice.

I went outside where the men stood. Each wore only cutoff jeans and shoes. Bob had a snow-white towel slung around the back of his neck. His teeth matched the color of the towel, making his tanned chest and shoulders look even darker. I swallowed hard.

"I'll show you the swimming hole." I started down the trail.

"What do you kids do for entertainment around here?" Dave asked.

"There's lots to do. My brother and I trap during the winter. Fish, swim, hunt and work in the field and garden in the summer. We climb the mountains, go hiking. And then there's always schoolwork."

We had reached the slough where Gay and John were already swimming. I turned to leave.

"Aren't you going swimming?" Dave grabbed my arm.

"Melody's a skinny-dipper." Gay giggled and tossed her head. Somehow she'd managed to keep her hair dry.

"Is that right?" Dave laughed.

"I've got school work to do." I freed my arm and scurried up the bank and into the field.

When they returned to the cabin an hour later, I was still reading. After changing into dry clothes in the chalet, the men came in for some hot cocoa. I peeked over the top of my text and watched Bob take a big gulp from the mug Mom handed him. His eyes were really more blue than hazel.

"John says he and Melody trap during the winter." Dave dried his hair with a towel.

"And they're both crack shots with a rifle, too. Melody got her first caribou when she was twelve years old. Last year John shot a black bear and Melody skinned and tanned it all by herself."

Even before Mom finished her speech, I felt warm and looked back into my text.

After they had left, I watched Gay bring a box of brush rollers out of a dresser rawer and put them on the table in front of her. Then she positioned a small mirror on the table.

I put my text down. "Doesn't it hurt to sleep on those things?"

"Not after you get used to it. Besides, it's worth having my hair look nice."

"Do you think you have enough curlers so that I could try it? I want to look nice for Dad tomorrow too."

"You've got to wash that filthy hair of yours first. No roller of mine in going on your head until then."

"Okay." I filled up the teakettle and pulled it to the hottest part of the wood stove.

Gay helped me wash and rinse in the basin. Then she applied the brush rollers while my hair was still wet.

"We'll let your hair dry overnight and tomorrow it will be beautiful." She took a towel off my shoulders.

I tossed in bed all night, unable to get comfortable. I even wakened myself several times by pulling at the bristly rollers. By morning all the curlers hung loose and askew.

"Ouch," I winced and pulled away from Gay when she attempted to take the first one out. "That hurt."

"You've twisted your hair around inside these brushes until they're a tangled mess. I'll be lucky if I can get them out without using a scissors."

"You'd better not cut my hair." I moved away.

"Stay still or I'll have to. The more you jerk like that the more tangled it's going to get."

I sat as still as possible, tears rolling down my cheeks until Gay finally freed all the rollers. Then she brushed and combed my hair.

"See? What did I tell you?" she said as I looked into the small mirror.

"It's pretty, isn't it?" I moved the mirror back and forth. "Get the other mirror so I can see the back of my head."

"And if you learn to keep your fingers out of your hair at night the rollers won't get tangled like they did this time." She held the other mirror behind me.

"What do you think, Mom?" I asked.

"It's just lovely. Dad will really be surprised."

"Yeah." I turned back to the mirror.

An hour later my hair started losing some of its curl. By train time I had nothing to show for my night of misery.

"It's too long," Gay consoled me on the way to meet the train. "It won't take a curl."

"Yours does."

"But I've been curling my hair for years. It's trained."

"You mean I'm going to have to suffer with those curlers in my head every night for years before I can have hair like yours?"

"There is another way." Gay stood by me at the train station as the family waited. "We could cut your hair. If it's shorter it will hold a curl longer."

"I'm not sure I want to do that."

"Your hair will grow back."

"But it's taken me five years to get it to grow this long from the last time Mom cut it."

"It didn't take that long. Look at your hair." She lifted a hank of it near the front of my face. "It's breaking off constantly and it's just full of split ends."

"So what?"

"So if you cut it, your hair will grow back healthier, prettier and faster."

"You think so?" I studied the lock of hair.

"Sure it will."

"I'll have to think about it," I said as the train appeared around the south bend.

CHAPTER 19
Close to Home

"I don't understand why you quit now, Leon." Mom jammed a piece of stove wood into the firebox when we got back to the cabin. "We were just getting our heads above water. Another year at that job and we would have had plenty of time and money to build the house."

"But Adak is so far away. I didn't come up here to be separated from the family."

"Maybe you should have thought about that before you decided to drag the whole family out here to the bush."

"We've got most of our winter supplies in already and I can start work on the house tomorrow. Then maybe when winter comes I can find another job closer to home. That way I can at least get home over the weekends."

"Okay." Mom sat down. "We'll just take it a day at a time."

Dad got up early that next morning and took the Cat up to the excavation Mr. Ihly had made three years before. John went with him. I helped Gay and Mom peel logs. Before noon, Dad drove the Cat back from the hill and shut it down behind the cabin.

"It's no good." He came over to us. "Our Cat is just not heavy enough to push those big boulders around. "We're going to have to build someplace else, and do without a basement."

Mom pulled a long strip of bark from one of the logs, pausing to sit down on another. "Why don't we just build onto what we already have?"

"If we did, we'd do it so eventually the original cabin could be torn down. It's not going to last through many more winters anyhow." Dad looked back at the sagging structure.

"Let's go see how it can be done." Mom stood and walked with Dad over to the house.

I hopped my way through the logs and followed my parents.

"If we build on this side we'll have to tear down the lean-to wood shed," Mom said as they walked to the right hand side of the cabin.

"That shed never stored enough wood for winter anyhow. And we should have one big enough to put the Cat under instead of letting it sit out in the snow with just a tarp over it all the time."

"Where would you put the new shed?" Mom looked around.

"Right over there." Dad walked farther out from the right hand side of the cabin, well into the trees. "Far enough away from the cabin to give us room to build the new house on this side, but close enough once the house is built to be convenient. I'll start digging post holes for the support logs today. In a week we can tear that old lean-to off the cabin and start hauling the wood into the new shed."

I ran back to Gay and John with the plans I'd heard. But when I rounded the other side of our little cabin I saw Dave talking to them. He held a large red canister on his shoulder. I looked around for Bob and felt disappointed but also relieved at the same time that he wasn't there.

"We've got company," I called back to Mom and Dad.

"Dave brought a fire extinguisher for the cabin," Gay said as they approached. "And he wants to know if we can come up to the railroad gang cars tonight to see a movie."

"Can we go?" John asked.

"Yeah. Can we?" I begged. The last movie I'd seen was during my trip into town. And even that was on television.

"I don't see why not." Mom looked back at our guest.

"Great." Dave swung the cannister to the ground. "The cook is making plenty of popcorn, so don't fill up on dinner."

I didn't. After we had eaten, Gay took her box of curlers off the shelf.

"Do you think that if you put my hair up in rollers now it would be curled by tonight?"

"I'd have to wet it down for it to take a curl at all. Your hair would never dry in time," she said between some bobby pins clutched in her teeth. "Unless we cut it." She looked up.

"But I like my hair long."

"Look at it. It just hangs there."

I got up and went to the mirror, studying my hair up close. "Okay. You can cut it. But only a little."

"Good." Gay finished her hair then found the hair shears. "Put some newspaper under the chair and a towel over your shoulders."

"Promise not to cut it too short?" I did as she said.

"Only enough to get rid of the split and broken ends."

I sat down and waited, hearing the shears at work. A big glob of my hair fell onto the newspaper.

"Not too much!" I jerked away.

"Will you sit still? You just made me take a big hunk right out of the middle of your head."

I sat and Gay cut. Finally she put the scissors down and wiped the clinging hair from my shoulders.

"Can I look now?"

"No. Not yet. I'm going to wet it down and put it up in rollers. If you sit with your head in the oven it just might dry before movie time."

Again, I sat. When my hair finally dried it was time to get dressed. Gay loaned me her green long sleeved pullover sweater as well as a small heart shaped locket necklace. I slipped into my snuggest fitting jeans, then spent a long time combing my hair until it was just right.

I took so long, in fact, that Gay and John started out before I was done. I ran barefoot up the trail, careful not to disturb my hair. And when I caught up with the others they were almost to the section house. By the time we had reached the gang cars, Bob stepped out into the mess car door opening. His frame was backlighted by the lights within. I sucked in a deep breath of air and maneuvered myself in front of John and Gay just as Bob extended a helping hand to me. I swallowed, extended my own hand, and began climbing the two metal rung stairs. Bob took my elbow and with a strong yet gentle guidance, helped me climb aboard.

"You're looking special tonight," he said in a low voice.

My eyes locked on his and for a split-second I couldn't find my voice.

"C'mon, Melody. Move." John who had crawled in by himself, prodded me from the rear.

I shifted my eyes, took a step to the side and knocked over one of the folding chairs that had been set up for the show. Then Bob helped Gay who glided in gracefully. I turned to the rows of chairs. They were set up two on each side of a center aisle. In front, someone had hung a white sheet for a movie screen. I selected one of two empty chairs on the left hand side of the aisle and slid into the window seat. Behind me Gay talked to Dave and Bob. John hovered around the large popcorn bowl. Minutes later both Gay and Dave passed me. Dave held two popcorn bowls. They sat in the left front row with Gay near the aisle. I sneaked a peek behind me. Bob was headed down the aisle, a popcorn bowl in each hand! I looked at the white sheet and held my breath.

"Would you like some popcorn?"

"Thank you." I turned and reached out.

"Don't mention it." He released the bowl into my hand then went up front and sat down across from Gay.

"When does the show start?" John plopped next to me, crunching popcorn in my ear.

"Right now." The cook shouted from behind the projector. "Will one of you kids hit the lights up there?"

"Didn't you hear him?" John reached in front of me when I didn't move. He flicked a switch on the wall next to my shoulder.

The movie had just started, but I dearly wanted to go home.

CHAPTER 20
Fire!

"Close the door! You'll chill my bread." Gay covered the few steps to the stove and pushed the rising bowls into the open oven.

"Sorry." I unwrapped a protective scarf from my mouth and nose. "Boy, is it ever cold out there." I pinched my eyelashes and pulled the frost off.

"Get anything?" John looked up from a comic book.

"Nothing is moving in this cold. It must be 40 degrees below zero out there." I poured a cup of coffee and wrapped my fingers around the warm mug.

Gay hovered around her bread a few more minutes then sat down. I took a seat also. The soft glow of our kerosene lamp gave the cabin a cozy feeling. I was happy to be back inside after the ten mile trapline run with Spook and looked around now, soaking up atmosphere.

Before Dad had left to work for the railroad as a cook on Dave's and Bob's gang, we'd finished off the woodshed and used the remaining logs to begin the addition. We ran out of logs before we did time, and Dad had decided with the few weeks he had left before reporting for work that fall that we should get the rest of our winter supplies in.

Both lofts above me now brimmed full of flour, sugar and beans. Stored under the beds and on shelves were store-bought canned goods. And in the chalet we had our usual selection of garden products. In the corner by the door stood the huge red fire extinguisher.

Dave had been up to visit a few times over the winter, and when he did, Mom always had John go up to Botner's house and start the furnace fire so Dave would have a place to sleep. That fire was going now, but not because we expected a visit from Dave. Instead, Bob was coming. He would be arriving on the early morning train and after his visit was going to return to Santa Barbara and college. I had already decided to avoid his hazel-blue eyes as much as possible. But he wasn't coming to see me anyway, I knew that.

"How much longer before we can open the door and cool this place down. I'm broiling to death." I peeled off my wool socks.

"It won't be much longer. Why don't you get into your nightgown like Mom and I did. You'll be cooler." Gay put more wood in the stove. She had her hair in curlers again, something I'd not bothered with.

I went over to my bed, grabbed my night clothes off of it and changed. Then I walked over to the big standard Underwood typewriter, inserted a piece of paper and tapped on a few keys. I was expecting my typing course to come any day and had been practicing for it.

"Do you have to peck at that thing?" John looked at me from the comic book again.

"No, I guess not. I was just trying it out." I picked up a weasel hide on a nearby stretching board and blew at the soft white fur. We'd been moderately successful with that year's trapline. The bridge gauge money was enough to buy some new traps. But we still only had the one #3. So far we'd caught three wolverine in it. John had been there for all of them.

Gay put her cinnamon rolls into the oven now, turning the hot loaves of bread out to cool on an oven rack that straddled the kitchen sink. "Last batch is in the oven." She removed her mitt. "We can open the door now."

John jumped up and swung the cabin door wide. Invading cold air rushed inward as hot escaping clouds billowed in the opposite direction.

"That's enough. I don't want to freeze to death," I yelled.

"It's time to check the furnace up at Botner's place anyway." John shut the door. "I'm going up there so I can cool down."

My brother grabbed his coat and scarf. When he left, I went to his bunk and laid down. Even in the back corner though, I found it still too hot to sleep. I tossed and turned trying to get into a comfortable position. My mind wandered to Gay and Dave. Last fall Dave had told Gay about a job that was coming open the next summer on the dining car of the passenger train. She was thinking about applying for it. She had it all figured out how she could live with Mrs. Ihly in town over the summer and do her school work in the evenings. She could see Dave more often that way too.

I turned onto my stomach now, pulling a pillow over my head.

"Do you smell smoke?" I surfaced a few minutes later.

"I just put some more wood in the stove." Gay glanced back toward it. "Holy Cow!"

Both Mom and I sat up and followed her stare. The cardboard lined ceiling in the front half of the loft rippled with tiny smoke waves. Then it burst into multicolored flames.

"Get the fire extinguisher!" Mom shouted.

Gay ran to the door while I unfolded the loft ladder. Mom poured a bucket of water into the firebox. "It's a chimney fire," she shouted.

Halfway up the ladder now, I reached down and grabbed the heavy extinguisher Gay raised to me. I heaved the cannister upside down, smashed the activator button in and layered a white foam on the flames.

"You've got it," Mom yelled up to me. "A little more near the chimney."

I shifted my aim just as the ladder rung snapped under the extra weight. I dropped the extinguisher, grabbing wildly as I fell.

"Is it out?" I jumped up, coughing.

"No." Gay threw a pot full of water at the ceiling. It came back down, drenching the front of her nightgown and hair. "We can't reach the fire from here. We're going to have to try from the roof."

I ran to my bunk, pulled on a pair of jeans, grabbed a coat and slipped my bare feet into a pair of bunny boots.

"I'll climb up on top. You start a bucket brigade."

Mom was wiping foam from the extinguisher off her glasses as I passed.

Shinnying up the front corner post of the addition, I crawled up onto the snow covered roof of the cabin. The pipe came free easily when I grasped it to steady myself.

"Here," Gay shouted from the corner of the cabin.

Cautiously, I made my way down the incline and reached for the upraised bucket. I grasped the bail then carried the bucket to the hole where smoke billowed. I tried splashing the water up into the rafters hoping to saturate the burning cardboard. My hands froze to the metal bail and bottom rim of the bucket. I ripped them free and let the container roll off the roof.

"Here's another one," Gay yelled.

"I need some gloves." I held my hands under my armpits.

"Here, take mine." She put the bucket down, tore off her mittens and threw them to me.

This time the trip up to the hole wasn't as easy. I slid on frozen water then again emptied the contents. Gay was outside with another bucket now and I slid down to where she waited.

"Try to throw it up into the fire," she yelled.

"I am trying. I can't reach it from up here, either."

"Just keep trying." She disappeared.

The bucketful of water went streaming through the same as the others. I could barely keep balance on the ice underfoot.

"Here," Gay called. This time she held a soaking wet wool blanket. "This is the last of the water. Try to poke the blanket up into the roof and smother the fire."

I grabbed the blanket's edge and dragged it behind me while climbing on my hands and knees. Head turned from the smoke, I took a deep breath, closed my eyes tightly and pushed the blanket inside. I could feel heat on my hands and tried to shove the wet wool upward into the log rafters.

"I lost it," I shouted back down to Gay who hadn't returned inside the cabin this time.

"Never mind. Come on down." She disappeared.

By the time I got down, Gay and Mom struggled in the doorway with one of the larger chest of drawers. I helped them carry the piece of furniture into a nearby snowbank, then followed them back inside the cabin. The smoke was thick and blue. I could hear crackling overhead. A blob of firey sugar dripped through the ceiling of the front loft, splattering on the floor near my right foot. I stomped it out and looked around. Where were my school books? On the shelves? Table?

I spotted Dad's typewriter, grabbed it up and rushed to the door, setting it down near the front of the cabin. Gay passed me, Ren in her arms. Mom was right behind her with an arm full of clothes and the can of silver dollars. I took a deep breath and plunged back inside. There were too many sugar fires to bother with now. I spotted some of my books and grabbed them up in an armload of other things, including the weasel pelt. The typewriter bell sounded loudly.

"Will you get that thing out of the way?" Gay passed me again.

I picked up the typewriter. The ribbon spewed out the top and dragged along the trail behind me. By the time I got back, Mom and Gay stood outside.

"My flute," Gay was saying. "I know right where it is. I'll go right to it and be back."

"No. It's too late." Mom shook her head.

"Mom, I know right where it is!" Gay insisted and cracked the door open only slightly.

Smoke billowed out as she lunged forward, then backed away coughing.

"It's no good. Let's start moving these things back from the cabin or they'll burn too." Mom closed the door.

We worked silently. The cabin looked strangely dark. Except for an occasional popping sound, I wouldn't have suspected what was happening inside.

"C'mon. Let's get some clothes out of the chests and put them on in the chalet." Mom grabbed Gay's arm.

I followed them to the chest of drawers. We'd saved the kerosene lamp and used it now to search the snow for clothes. My jeans legs were caked with ice, but I didn't feel cold. Gay and Mom left for the chalet with the lamp and their bundles while I watched flames lick out the mylar windows. Spook began to whine. I walked over to the big dog, petted him and watched spellbound as sparks began working their way through the roof. They floated lazily to greet the dark starlit sky.

"Mom! Gay! Melody!" I heard John screaming.

"Don't let him go inside the cabin!" Mom ran from the chalet.

I saw him now, coming down the section house trail. He stumbled over his snowshoes, slipped out of them, and stumbled again. Then we were all together, crying.

"I thought you were in there...I thought you were in there," John's sobs poured out. Flickering light from the cabin found our little circle.

"We're all okay." Mom said the words over and over again as an explosion of ammunition sent a column of flame shooting straight through the tarpapered roof into a now lighted sky.

Chapter 21
The Waiting Game

"I know you want to give your guests a warm welcome but this is carrying things a bit too far." Bob stood in a burned area where less than a day before he could have sat in a kitchen chair.

Gay giggled and dug through the warm ashes with a stick in search of salvageable items. We were all tired and rummy from the experience which had left us homeless, and even as we shoveled snow on the flames while our cabin burned down, had made jokes. It seemed right somehow that the little cabin in which we'd experienced so much joy and pain be given an appropriate wake.

In the few hours after the time we'd said our final eulogies over the cremated remains and daylight the following morning, Gay had uncurled her singed hair and taken a skimpy sponge bath with the small amount of snow we'd gathered and melted on the stove at Botner's house. I hadn't found any clean clothes, so put on my smoky ones.

"How'd it start?" Bob wanted to know.

"Gay was baking again." John skirted a pile of hot ashes, went over to the range and tried to open the oven door.

"Last time she baked something we had an earthquake that wiped half of Alaska off the map," my brother teased.

With Bob's help, they wrestled the oven door free and we peered inside. The pan was there but it held nothing.

Does anyone know how it started?" Bob didn't bother to close the sagging door.

"We know it had something to do with the chimney. Mom thinks that a small quake we had a few weeks ago may have shaken a section of the pipe loose. Then all we needed was a good chimney fire. The flames leapt out of the pipe and into the cardboard lined ceiling of the cabin. By the time we saw it, the roof on the whole right side of the front loft was on fire."

"Didn't the fire extinguisher help at all?"

"It started to, but Melody dropped it."

Bob glanced up at me, his eyes twinkled as he made little chastising noises against the roof of his mouth with his tongue.

"The ladder broke." I worked my stick deeper into some dead ashes.

"What matters is that all of you got out of this without a scratch."

"It'll take more than a little fire to knock us out." John threw a charred timber into a pile of smoldering wood.

"Hey, guess what I found." Gay pulled something from the pile of ashes on the far side of us and held up a blob of ash–clinging metal. "I think it's my flute."

Bob walked through the cinders towards her. His footsteps puffed up the fine residue surrounding us.

"You should take better care of your things." He turned the blob over and over in his mittened hands before giving it back to her.

"The thing never played in tune anyhow." She dropped the remains and they disappeared back down into the soft ash.

We dug for more buried treasure, recognizing the twisted skeletal parts of something here or there. Then we loaded the sled with clothes and food from the chalet and prepared for the mile journey to Botner's house. John, who took the last minute before we left to rummage through some open chest of drawers in a snowbank, came running towards us, a bulging sock swung from his hand.

"I knew it was a good idea to take this money out from under my bunk." He grinned.

I couldn't say the same. My collection of money for traps, most of my school books, even my completed general science final exam had burned. I watched John stuff the sock into his parka pocket then turned and gave Spook the "get–up" command. He and little Papeete started up the trail with their sled loaded. The typewriter was balanced precariously on top and its bell rung with every bump in the trail on the trip home. The cold snap had persisted through the night and by the time we reached Botner's house our thighs were numb. Last inside, I peeled off my outer garments and shivered as warmth from the wood stove in the kitchen found the chilled marrow of my bones.

"There's a cup of cocoa on the table for you." Mom looked up from the pancake batter she poured onto a hot griddle.

I hung my coat on a nearby peg in the wall and joined Gay, John and Bob who already sipped the hot contents of their cups. The cocoa warmed me inside and the cooking pancakes smelled good.

None of us had gotten much rest since long before the fire. After Bob arrived, we'd all tried sleeping for the few hours until daylight. But I, along with Gay and Mom, kept smelling smoke. We passed each other several times during the night checking the kitchen range and downstairs furnace until finally deciding to stay up.

I stared into the cocoa in front of me and watched its lazy swirl of steam rise upwards while John recounted his experience of the night before. He'd thought he was watching a spectacular display of the northern lights, until he got close enough to home to know better.

"I'm really not hungry." I pushed my plate of pancakes away. "While the rest of you are up watching the stove fires, I'm going to get some sleep." I walked past the bathroom, into one of the two bedrooms, and lay down on the double bed.

"Melody, take your clothes off and get under the covers," Mom's voice drifted toward me.

Ren's playful barking wakened me a few hours later. I sat up abruptly, then remembering where I was, lay back down and listened to voices coming from the kitchen. We'd called Mrs. Ihly and told her about the cabin. Now all we could do was wait for the train and Dad to get home. The talk was bothersome so I came out of the bedroom.

"Melody, why don't you go through all the school books and figure out what needs reordering. The rest of us are ready for some sleep now," Mom said.

Left alone in the kitchen with the remains of scattered syllabuses and water–damaged text books, I started the list. Gay and I could share the biology and literature texts until a replacement came. But my world history text was missing. Most of the syllabuses were unreadable and all of the tests were gone. None of John's books had survived. I would have to order a make–up exam for both John and my finals which would be taken without the benefit of another review of our semester's work. It would have been easier to list what we'd saved instead of lost. But I completed the order, then sat at the table with my arms folded and head down.

When I awoke, the evening darkness had settled. I stood quietly then walked over to the living room entrance where a floor grid still sent a faint flow of heat up from the basement furnace. I sneaked quietly through the living room where Bob and John slept, made a turn to the right, then again turned and opened the door leading to the basement. I took a few steps down the wooden stairway and closed the basement door behind me. We kids had been inside this house enough during the last two years to know it by heart. When my feet hit the concrete slab at the base of the steps, I knew the broad side of the furnace was directly to my right. To my left, I heard dripping water. I stepped around that way onto a gravel drainage area and made a wide arc which took me back underneath the wooden stairs and to the furnace door.

Botner said he'd made the house with a flat roof intentionally so that he could tap rain and snow runoff through the pipe which ran from the roof to the basement. The idea worked to a certain degree. He did get plenty of water from summer rains and melting snow. But once the flow started, it couldn't be shut off. Instead the overflow was directed to the gravel filled area where it drained away. This alway gave the basement a damp, mildew smell. Also, the water caught in the drum had a yellowish tinge and tarpaper odor. It came in handy for laundry, baths, and washing dishes, but it couldn't be used for cooking, so a trip to Gold Creek was necessary.

I reached out, opened the furnace door with the end of a huge poker and swung the door wide. Red coals illuminated the area around me and little flames erupted as I added one more piece of wood. I cursed upon burning the back of my right hand against the open cast iron door.

"Need help?" Bob's form was softly outlined in the firelight where he stood about halfway down the plank stairs.

"No. I've got it." I put my stockinged foot on the end of another piece of wood and shoved it inside. "There's not going to be any light down here when I close this thing," I warned.

"I'm not afraid of the dark. Are you?" Bob took another step downward.

I hesitated, then slammed the door. Slowly, quietly, I made my way under the steps, around the dripping water drum, onto the slab, and climbed the first stair in the dark.

"You get lost?" Bob sat at the kitchen table, smiling when I finally came back upstairs. Gay, who had somehow found time to take a bath and change into clean clothes, was there also. I poured a cup of coffee and went to the bedroom. There was a pile of clothes on the floor near the end of the bed and I rummaged through it searching for some clean jeans, shirt and underwear. I found what I wanted and quickly peeled out of my old clothes. It was then I caught a glimpse of myself in the full-length mirror on the back of the bedroom door. We never had a mirror that big at the cabin. The bean pole frame, with its big hands and feet, gawked back at me. Instead of getting dressed, I slipped into my nightgown and crawled into bed.

Gay wakened me from a fitful sleep sometime later that night. I watched her from a small cave formed in the blankets as she undressed by moonlight that streamed through the window.

"What time is it?"

"We just got back from meeting the train. We got a Northwind from Madge saying Dad would be home on the freight train early this morning." She crawled under the covers. "That Bob is so crazy. My sides are aching from laughter."

"He likes you."

"He likes all girls."

"I mean he likes you a lot."

"Bob? He's just a fun guy, that's all. Now go back to sleep. I'm tired." She rolled over.

I laid there with my eyes open, watching the moonlight cast flickering shadows from nearby trees onto the ceiling. Then, remembering the dream Gay had wakened me from, closed my eyes and tried to force myself back into it.

"Dad's home!" I sat up in bed, shaking Gay.

"I saw Madge and brought the groceries you ordered." Dad talked to Mom as we ran into the kitchen. "She said Dr. Maddock insisted he would be up this Saturday to see for himself that all of you are okay," he continued. "How is this place set for stove wood?"

"Not too well. I was going to have the kids start hauling it up from our place tomorrow."

"When it gets daylight Bob and I will go out and saw enough trees to last for awhile. Since the kids won't have schoolwork to worry about for a few weeks, they can all help."

By Saturday the wood shed was full. And true to his word, Dr. Maddock arrived carrying his medical bag. He brought with him several huge boxes of groceries, and a large envelope the conductor had given him to deliver to us. It turned out to be filled with money – a collection taken up by nameless railroad workers and homesteaders who'd heard about the fire.

When we finally got around to our physicals, I took my turn sitting on the edge of the bed while Dr. Maddock tapped at my knee with a rubber hammer. He looked into my ears and eyes, then listened to my heart.

"Did you get burned anywhere?"

"No." I shook my head.

"What's this?" He picked up my right hand, directing his attention to the back.

"That happened when I was stoking the furnace in the basement the other night."

"I'll put some salve on it." He reached in his bag.

"Dr. Maddock?" I said meekly.

"Hmmmm?" He opened the lid on a small tube filled with white ointment.

"Am I okay?"

"You're in excellent health. Excellent." He rubbed the ointment in.

"I mean am I okay, you know, as a girl?"

"Oh." His glasses slipped slightly down his nose as he looked at me. "How old are you?"

"I turned fifteen three weeks ago."

"And you haven't..."

"No." I thought now that asking him hadn't been such a good idea.

"You'll be okay." He patted my knee.

"But my sisters..."

"That doesn't mean a thing. Some girls mature later is all."

"How long?" I buttoned my shirt.

"A half–year at the most." He twisted the lid back on the little tube, deposited it into his black bag and snapped it shut. "You'll be fine."

THE WAITING GAME

The next morning I followed last in line as we went to the train to see Bob and Dr. Maddock off. A light snowfall danced around Gay and Bob when the train rounded the bend. Then, as the train pulled past me and slowed to a stop, I saw Bob lean slightly towards Gay. With fists clenched inside my mittens I turned away as he approached. He kissed me lightly on the cheek.

"You keep that trapline checked, all right?" Bob smiled.

I still clenched my fists as he boarded and waved. The train moved away in swirling snow mixed with brake steam.

Right then, a half-year seemed like a long time to wait.

CHAPTER 22
Bearded Knight

It was a tradition in our family to greet the New Year by burning a bough from the Christmas tree at midnight. It was then we all made our New Year's resolutions. Because of the fire, which had destroyed the spruce bough decoration Gay had made in the old cabin, our ceremony that New Year had been premature and resolutions were the furthest thing from my mind. But it wasn't long after the beginning of the year that Mom and Dad called a family meeting in the kitchen. Mom stood, back to the stove, arms folded. The rest of us sat at the kitchen table. I listened while rolling up an edge of a page in my notebook with my left index finger.

"What I'm saying is should we rebuild knowing that we are under no obligation to? We have our land cleared and have fulfilled the requirements to apply for our patent," Dad continued the conversation.

"But I want to stay here. I don't want to move to town," Gay said.

"Me neither." John looked up.

"Sure, that's fine for you to say. But I'm thinking of Mom. She's been out here four years. I think the time has come for her to have a say in this thing." Dad looked at her.

"The children should have some say," Mom spoke.

"Yes, they should. But remember if we rebuild, you're going to be the one stuck here in a big empty house in a few years when they're all gone."

"I'm never leaving." John looked down.

"The kids will be around for a long time. At least Melody will." Mom looked at me and I nodded.

"True. Melody will probably be here another three years. Then what? You're stuck up here all by yourself and I'm working on a railroad gang somewhere hundreds of miles away."

"That situation won't change if we move to the city, unless you get a job right where we live."

"We can look into that too."

"And what about the children's schoolwork?" Dad started again.

"At the rate they're going, they'll never finish."

"I'm not that far behind," I mumbled. "And if the cabin hadn't burned down..."

"But it did burn down," Dad interrupted. "And now that it has I think we should seriously consider moving into town where you kids can go to public school and Mom and I don't have to hound you every minute about the importance of your high school educations."

"That's just great." Gay wiped her eyes. "I'm going to be eighteen and in the tenth grade. Do you realize how far behind that puts me? I'll be going to classes with kids younger than Melody."

"I've got to agree, Leon," Mom said. "We pulled the kids out of the city where they were well established in a school system, dragged them out here in the bush to do correspondence school and because of the work involved in keeping the homestead, they've gotten behind in their studies. Now you want to uproot them again, take them from a place that is rightfully part theirs because of all the work they've put into it and set them back into a school system where they'll be three years behind others their ages."

"What do you want me to tell you, Alice? That moving up here was a mistake in the first place? Okay, to the extent that the children haven't taken advantage of the opportunity correspondence school presented to them, it was, and I'm sorry. But we can't go on crying over spilt milk the rest of our lives."

"I'm not crying over spilt milk. I just think that since the children were affected most by the move up here, which like myself they had no say over, that this time they should have a say."

"Fine. The four of you decide and I'll go along with what you say." Dad stood.

"Now, wait just a minute." Mom held out a hand. "You're not just going to walk away from this whole decision scot free."

"I don't know what else I can say, Alice. I've stated my point of view. Now it's time, with all the facts in front of us, for you to decide."

"No. It's time for us to decide. You wanted to come up here so the family could be together, discuss these things and come to united decisions. So we're going to do just that."

"I just wanted us to be together. That's all I wanted when we moved up here. I wanted the kids to get a family experience that other children don't even begin to get anymore. But it didn't turn out that way."

"I think I've had a great childhood," I spoke.

Dad looked at me. "It's over."

"Maybe for Sandra and Gay, but not for me. I'm just as old now as Sandra was when we first came to Gold Creek."

"And she hated it, as did your Mother."

"But I don't. This is my home. This is where I want to live. I'm even going to stay here after I'm eighteen and trap for a living."

"Okay." Dad put his hands on the table. "So everybody wants to live here but nobody wants to cooperate."

"We cooperate." Gay still wiped her eyes.

"Didn't you just tell me you were three years behind in school? And how about John, two years behind. Melody is at least a half-year behind. You call that cooperation?"

I grabbed a tissue from the box on the table.

"That's not fair." Mom stepped in. "If these children had been given some decent supervision that year I was in town, they never would have slipped this far behind in the first place."

"You've been here the last two years," Dad said. "Have you noticed they don't do anything they don't want, no matter what you do to encourage or force them?"

"All I know is that if I'd been forced to go to a public school all these years I would have failed and probably ended up in trouble because school bores me," John said.

"Out here I can do things that interest me. I can work in the field, fix the chain saw and equipment. I don't see how diagramming a sentence or learning about how far the sun is from the earth is going to help me get a job when I'm an adult."

"I don't care how much practical knowledge you've got." Mom shook her head. "You'll never get inside the door of a good employer unless you've got that diploma."

"Then I'll finish school. But I'll do it out here."

"What if we promise to work real hard at our school lessons?" Gay's eyes were red but dry.

"How do any of you, most of all you, plan to do that?" Dad said. "You have a job this summer. You're not even going to be around here to do school."

"It's only a summer job. I'll take my school books with me into town and study on my days off and at night."

"That sounds good, but it won't happen." Dad shook his head.

"I'll study hard," I said.

"We should at least give the children a chance to prove they can go through with this if they want to," Mom added.

"They've had their chance, Alice. None of them are going to finish high school out here before they're eighteen and once that happens they'll leave you holding the bag."

"I don't mind living out here any more." Mom shrugged.

"Don't you think you've sacrificed enough in your lifetime for the sake of what others want? Why don't you do what you want for a change?" Dad took a deep breath. "What I'm saying is 'here's your chance'. We've been handed a clean slate to start on all over again. And this time I'm not going to be the one to make the decision."

Dad stopped. We children looked at Mom.

"Do we have to decide this thing today?" She turned and pulled a teakettle to the front of the stove.

"If you want more time to think this over, fine." Dad stood again. "Just consider one more thing. Where am I going to find time to build a new home out here if I'm working this far away all the time?"

"I guess we'd find the time now just like you were going to find it before the cabin burned down." Mom turned back to face Dad.

"Okay. I give up. I'm catching the train back to work tonight and the next time I come home we'll discuss this further." Dad put on his coat and left.

"Does that mean we're going to stay?" John asked.

"I don't know." Mom shook her head. "I just don't know anymore."

That night, after Dad said goodbye to Mom, the rest of us went with him to meet the train. Once in Anchorage, Dad would have to hitch-hike, fly or catch a freight going down to Seward. Lately Dad had spent more time traveling to get home than he actually spent there. But at least he'd been home several times since the fire and over the holidays.

While we waited for the train, I studied the vaguely moonlit shadows of the surrounding mountains. My mind wandered from hunting those mountains and picking the sweet large blueberries nestled down into different colored tundra moss, to the trapline and my plans for trapping enough pelts to make parkas for the family. So far we had a good collection of smaller pelts, but beaver sets were hard work. Wolverine had been easy to lure into our sets. But we never held them very long in our smaller traps.

I turned my back to a south winter wind and scanned the tree line to the north, waiting for a reflection from the oncoming train's headlight. Instead, I picked out a small beam of light alongside the tracks. I kicked the toe of my left bunny boot against the heel of my right to warm the numbing toes hidden inside and watched the beam come closer. The man wore mukluks, jeans, an old gray wool jacket and a trapper's hat with the ear flaps tied down.

"Hello." The stranger beckoned us as he approached. "That train come through here yet?"

"Not yet," John said.

"That's good. I had a grocery order to put on and was afraid I wouldn't get here in time. You must be the Ericksons." He held out a hand to Dad, who took it. "I'm Ken. I'm looking after a cabin up by the creek for a friend of mine. Heard about the fire. That's a tough break. You're living up at Botner's place now?" he asked.

"For the time being. We really haven't decided what our next step will be."

"Well, if you need anything, just lean out the back door and give a holler. My cabin can't be more than a mile away." He scratched his neatly trimmed black beard. "Is one of you getting on the train?"

"I'm going into town."

"Would you mind making sure the baggageman gets this letter off at Talkeetna? I'm going to need some coffee real quick and don't want my order to go all the way to Anchorage."

"Sure. I'll see to it." Dad took the letter. "If you need some coffee to hold you over until your order comes, why don't you go back up with the kids after the train. Alice will give you some."

"I'll take you up on that. Tea is fine to drink in the afternoon, but nothing beats a cup of coffee in the morning."

After Dad got on the train, we sorted through the mail and walked with Ken back to Botner's place.

"Have you lived in Talkeetna long?" I asked.

"Most of my life. My Dad has a sawmill down there."

We had reached the house and once inside, Ken waited patiently as Mom scooped some coffee into a glass jar.

"Kenny's dad runs a sawmill in Talkeetna." Gay said as he took off his cap and mittens. I was surprised by the receding hairline.

"Really? What size operation does he have?"

"It's called a one–man saw mill. But it really takes three people to operate it comfortably. You've probably seen Botner's old sawmill. The one he used to cut all the lumber for this place. It's the same size as that." Ken accepted the jar. "You bought Carp's old place, didn't you?"

"That's right."

"Nice piece of property. Eric says he's not certain just what you're going to do now. Have you thought about rebuilding?"

"Not exactly. With Leon gone we'd have trouble getting in enough logs to finish off what we've started."

"I took the liberty of going down there." Ken put his cap on. "With what you've got up, you could easily convert to a board and batten house. You've got access to a saw mill to make lumber as well as plenty of river islands to harvest cottonwood and spruce." I waited for Ken to continue, but instead he picked up his mittens. "I'd best be getting back. The little place I'm staying in doesn't keep a fire very long and I don't want to have things freeze up."

"Well, come over when you can spend a little more time," Mom added.

"I'll do that." He nodded and opened the door. "Can I borrow a pair of snowshoes from you tonight? That way I can just cut through the woods to my place. It's faster than following the tracks."

A few seconds later I watched through the kitchen window as Ken selected a pair of shoes, dropped them onto the ground and quickly slipped into the bindings.

"Do you think maybe we could use that sawmill and make our own lumber from Cottonwood Island for the new house?" John asked.

"I don't know." Mom put the coffee away.

"Ken would probably run it for us and help build the house if you asked him. He said he had nothing to do while he was up here," Gay added.

"He is also up here to get away. I'm sure he doesn't want to get involved in cutting lumber and building a house. He probably gets plenty of that back in Talkeetna."

"Couldn't you talk to him about it? He did bring up the subject first," Gay urged.

"Okay. I'll see what can be done. But understand this. If we stay Dad is going to want to see some schoolwork getting done, and so am I."

We nodded eagerly.

CHAPTER 23
The Seed

At daybreak the next morning, John and I gathered our snares, ice pick and hatchet together, and headed for mile 267 on the railroad. We wanted to make our beaver sets at a swamp there before our new school books arrived. We sat in the sled, a new seven foot akhio Dad brought shortly after Christmas, and let both Spook and Papeete pull us down the trail that Ken had snowshoed the night before. We'd always wanted an akhio. It was a flat bottomed fiberglas sled that looked a lot like a toboggan, but the bottom sloped up gently around the entire perimeter. It reminded me of an oblong bowl. This type of sled was great for hauling wood and using on the trapline because it could carry a large load. The three small runners fastened tightly to the bottom of the akhio kept the entire bottom of the sled from contacting the snow and creating a lot of drag. Because of its design it swished easily along the trail. That morning, before reaching Ken's cabin, we got out of the sled and snowshoed a new trail in front of the dogs and toward the tracks. We joined the railbed just before the Susitna River bridge at mile 263.

With John in front of the sled and me running behind we both urged the dogs to cross as fast as possible. Papeete, for his small size, kept pace with Spook. He'd learned to run the bridge and after only a few cautious crossings had become so sure of his footing that he began to gain on Spook. Instead of the woolly coat that Spook had, Papeete's fur sported a glossy glow. But his mother had been a mix of husky, shepherd and lab so I hadn't thought much about it.

As Papeete began to grow though he didn't look that much like Spook in other ways. For instance, his ears didn't stand straight up like Spook's. Again I had excused this attribute because of his Labrador heritage. His eyes were brown, another fact I'd argued away. After all, blue eyes were recessive. I'd learned that from my biology course. One thing I couldn't dismiss so easily though was his size. Both Papeete's mother and Spook were large dogs, and now Papeete, having just passed his six month birthday, should have been showing a little more stature.

I couldn't argue about his lack of spirit though. For his dwarfed size, Papeete pulled his little heart out and although still a puppy, his fifty pounds of black midgetry was solid muscle and bone. Because of his willingness to pull, I just knew this had to be Spook's pup. The runt of the litter, maybe, but nonetheless Spook's offspring. And I'd believed that right up until a few weeks past when I'd seen our neighbor to the south. He was followed by a male, jet black cocker spaniel.

John and I got back into the sled and the dogs pulled us along at a trot. The middle of the tracks were packed solid with snow, and the sled glided along with little or no effort on their parts. At the mile 267 swamp, we made our set then headed the dogs for home.

"What's that over there?" John pointed to the left hand side of the tracks when we rounded the bend homeward with about three miles to go.

I followed his point and saw several ravens sitting in the snow around a large brown spot. "Looks like a moose kill." I hauled the dogs up short. "Let's go see."

The spot was only about a hundred feet from the tracks and in the trees. As soon as we started that direction Papeete caught the scent and began to lunge ahead of Spook in their single file hook–up.

"It's a train kill," John confirmed.

"The meat's no good now. Sure wish we could have found it a day earlier." I leaned down and grabbed the coarse brown fur along the back and pulled hard. It held fast.

"We could dress it out for dog food." John took off his snowshoes.

Papeete whined and licked his chops.

I checked my wrist watch. "Okay, but we'd better hurry. We're going to lose the sun pretty quick."

We slipped out of our shoes and began digging out the huge carcass. The animal had evidently died of an internal injury or been shot shortly after being hit. It remained partially standing on its long legs in the deep snow. We dug down far enough to free and cut the hooves off then turned the carcass on its back.

"Do you want to do the honors?" John handed me his sideknife.

"Only if you quarter it." I hesitated. "And take the head off."

"It's a deal." He slipped the butt of the knife in my hand.

The partly frozen condition of the animal protected us from the full effect of its ripeness. On occasion I'd get a whiff of the aroma that kept both Spook and Papeete whining anxiously.

John began working ahead of me by using a hatchet to split the rib cavity and remove the head. By the time I'd finished my job, we were ready to roll the animal on its side again and dump the offensive intestines. Then while I turned the sled around, John finished quartering the meat. We brought all the quarters to the tracks in four separate trips through the soft snow.

"Do you think they can pull that whole thing home in one trip?"

"We're sure going to make them try." John put the akhio in the middle of the tracks and together we piled the quarters inside.

"Get up." We both pushed on the load to help the dogs start the sled moving. Papeete jumped clear up into the air, throwing his weight against the harness. Spook, in a more dignified manner, expended as much effort. The sled didn't budge.

John pushed from the rear this time while I went to the front of the sled, grabbed onto a place in the tow line and gave the command. The dogs lunged. This time the sled inched forward slightly. Papeete's solid little muscles bulged under his shiny black fur.

"Keep it going. Keep it going," John urged.

The sled slowly gained momentum.

"Whatever you do, don't let them stop," John panted out and trotted behind.

"I just hope a train doesn't catch us in the middle of these tracks without warning. We'd never get off in time."

"Save your worrying for the bridge." John, having caught his breath, walked a quick pace alongside the steadily moving sled.

With a few minor hold–ups because of areas between the rails that had been dug out by the section crew in order for them to shim under the rails and minimize frost heave, we finally stopped near the approach of the bridge.

"We could take it across one quarter at a time," I said.

"No. That would take four times as long and it's getting dark. You know Mom. She'll be worrying soon."

I looked at the long span of bare ties ahead of us.

"The loaded sled isn't going to pull very easily over that."

"We'll get a running start at it." John leaned on the load and dug his feet in.

I stopped for one final listen for oncoming trains, then slowly started the sled moving again.

"Get up! Get up!" I yelled and pulled.

The dogs started going as fast as possible. We were on the north threshold. Snow still clung to the tops of these ties because there was no steel–girdered structure over them. Nevertheless the sled slowed while the dogs watched their footing. I ran alongside the sled outside of the rail on a narrow edge of extended ties. At the end of the threshold the dogs hit bare ties. They pulled the sled about twenty feet onto the main portion of the bridge before the loaded akhio behind squealed to a halt and jerked me backward.

"Get up! Get up!" John yelled from behind, pushing. The dogs pulled a few inches farther.

"It's no good. We'll never get this across in one load." I looked back at my brother.

"We're committed now. We can't turn this thing around to unload. It's just a couple of hundred yards before we hit the other threshold. We'll make it. This time when they get it moving, don't let them stop."

I attached a length of rope to the traces and wrapped it around my arms and waist several times. "Let's go get 'em, Papeete." I jerked on the rope.

Papeete lunged again and again against his harness. Spook leaned into his with all his mature strength. The sled began its chalk–board screech against the ties and I gritted my teeth.

"Keep going!" John yelled and pushed as we inched our way tie by tie towards the opposite end of the bridge.

My arms pulled from the shoulder sockets and toes curled downwards in my canvas mukluks as I latched them like hooks into the next spacing in the ties ahead of me. We kept the sled moving, every now and then hitting the briefest pocket of crumpled ice on top of several ties that would send us just a little farther forward. Finally we reached the south threshold, then solid packed snow between the rails on the opposite side.

In a few more minutes we were off the tracks and on that

morning's snowshoed trail. Our overflowing load dragged at the side of the trail and we again helped the dogs pull. We were at the house before dark, but when we opened the door Mom smelled us.

"What did you two get into now?"

"We brought back a thousand pounds of free dog food." John related the story, careful to leave out the part about the bridge.

"Well, bury it in the snow somewhere away from the house. Then come in here and take a bath."

We hauled our load to the outside of the nearby woodshed, dumped the quarters off, then unhitched the dogs. Spook lay happily in the snow, but Papeete, free of his harness, took off around the house at a full run, leaping through the deep snow in areas where there was no trail. Having circumnavigated the structure three times at top speed he stopped at his house, picked up his food pan and tossed it up into the air.

"That dog is plumb loco!" John laughed and hung up the harnesses in the shed. "I think he was holding out on us."

While John went inside the house, I still laughed and watched. Then I retrieved the double–bitted axe from the shed and in the settling dark began chopping a large portion of the frozen meat off one of the quarters for each of the dogs.

"Need help?"

I looked up to see Ken on a pair of snowshoes. He held our pair under his right arm.

"Nope. Just about finished."

"Is that a train kill?"

"Yeah. John and I just brought it down from 266. It's a bit ripe here and there, but the dogs don't mind." I threw one chunk to Spook, who grabbed it up in his huge mouth and trotted over to his dog house. Papeete dragged his in the same direction. "Come on in. We were just finishing up."

"Straight to the bathroom, young lady." Mom held her nose as we entered.

"It doesn't smell that bad," I heard Ken say as I closed the bathroom door behind me.

A few minutes later, washed up and wearing clean clothes, I re-entered the kitchen. Ken still stood with his coat on. John was grinning.

"Ken got two moose on the other side of the creek and asked us to help him clean and haul them in."

"You don't have to come along." Ken looked at me.

"I don't mind. The three of us can handle it faster than two of you."

"You'd better take a lantern," Mom said as Ken reached for the doorknob.

While Ken and John started ahead, I disturbed Spook and Papeete from their dinners and began hitching them up. Then, with a balancing rein in my left hand I stood in the middle of the akhio and gave the command.

Spook looked back at me, ears down. Then he finally led off after the two men.

CHAPTER 24
Old Ghosts

Ken sat drinking a cup of coffee at our house that Sunday morning in mid–February while we all listened to a series of radio shows. We always declared Sunday afternoons holidays from work so as not to miss the back–to–back line up of the Green Hornet, The Shadow and other half–hour radio shows. I sat at the opposite end of the table from Ken and halfway listened to the shows while doing my studies.

Mom and Dad had made an arrangement with Ken to help us rebuild. While preparing to relocate the old Botner sawmill down in Cottonwood Island, Ken had been over to our house almost every day since early January.

He and John had plowed a road through the snow to the island and prepared a place to set up the mill. They had already harvested some spruce trees which were now stacked and waiting the bite of the blade. Then they had plowed the road from our homestead, under the bridge and to the old mill which had to be dug out and fixed up. In a few more days they would pull the sawmill down to Cottonwood Island and we'd be in the milling business.

I took a piece of notebook paper from my binder, noting where I stood in my courses. The general science make–up exam had come through. And finally, I was officially out of the ninth grade. With general science out of the way, I'd succeeded in passing Gay who still had a ninth grade elective to complete. I knew I would have to hustle though if I were going to start the eleventh grade that fall. When I looked up from my notebook, Ken looked back down at the card game he was playing.

"I guess I'll go feed the dogs." I stood up.

Once outside, I walked the few feet in the dark to the shed, grabbed up the axe and by dim moonlight scraped snow off a quarter of the tainted meat.

"Need some light?" Ken came out of the house and turned on a flashlight with his mittened hand. He directed the small beam to the area where I chopped. A few seconds later I picked up the two chunks of frozen meat and stood up.

"Thanks."

"Any time." He redirected the beam to the trail in front of him and started homeward.

I threw the meat to the dogs, paused to watch him walk the trail to the cabin, then went back inside. The water in the teakettle was already hot so I picked it up and went into the bathroom. Botner's house provided a luxury we'd gotten used to very easily. It had an inside toilet, bathroom sink and a real bath tub. Earlier in the winter we'd had plenty of water for baths from the catchment system off the roof. But most of that snow had melted away, so we'd begun filling up the three large garbage cans with snow. We'd let them melt down and keep adding snow until the cans were full. Snow melting was a long involved process. A garbage can of packed snow melted down to only several gallons. Consequently we'd been sledding water up from the spring at our homestead to supplement it.

Even without running water, being able to let used water go down a drain and into a cesspool instead of taking it out in a slop pail had become an expected convenience. And although we still used the outhouse most of the time, an indoor toilet, flushed with a bucket of water, was an extravagant but welcome option on cold winter nights.

I dumped part of the teakettle's contents into the bathroom sink and with a towel wiped away the rising steam that stuck to the medicine cabinet. Goose bumps raised quickly as I sponged the warm soapy water over my skin.

I'm going to bed now and getting up early to do school," I called to my brother and sister as I exited the bathroom a few minutes later in my nightclothes. "Whoever is watching the fires then, be sure to wake me up before you go to bed."

Gay was the one who woke me and we both went out to the kitchen to study.

"You been to bed yet?" I asked.

"I tried and couldn't sleep." She placed the full cup of coffee on the table next to me then sat down. "Dave wants to get married."

"That doesn't surprise me. I've see you two necking on the couch when he comes up here to visit."

"He's ready for marriage now, and I'm not sure."

"Do you love him?"

"Yes. I'll never love anyone else like I love Dave."

"Then what's the problem?"

"I'm going to be eighteen and still in school for one thing. I haven't had a chance to be on my own yet. Besides, you know how Mom reacted when Sandra wanted to get married to Doug."

"That was different. Sandra was only sixteen." I flipped through my history text and Gay stopped talking for a minute.

"Sandra said she'd like for us to come up and visit soon."

"I don't want to visit Sandra."

"It would just be an overnight trip."

"I don't want to go visit her." I started reading my text.

I had seen Sandra over the past few years when she was on the train going to and from Chulitna but never did say more than 'hi' to her. She had one child and had lived at the Chulitna cabin since the summer of '63 while Doug left for jobs as far away as Amchitka Island. Gay had been the only one to keep in real touch with Sandra over the years. Mom and Dad rarely spoke of her at all, nor was Sandra spoken about in Mom's presence very often.

Gay started her school work, then in a few minutes checked the kitchen range fire. "I think I'll try to get some sleep," she said and left the room.

The Coleman lantern burned brightly on the table. Its buzzing sound annoyed me. I rubbed my face with my hands and sat back staring out the dark window only as far as reflection allowed. Then I stood up, put on my mukluks and coat and sneaked quietly outside.

I walked the road to the tracks using the flashlight only occasionally on the plowed out trail. When I reached the section house, I continued down to our homestead and stood in the ashes of our cabin. The small beam from the flashlight silhouetted the skeletal beam structure of the beginning of our new house. Ken and John had plowed the snow away from the area and made areas to stack lumber. I debated going down the Cat road through the field to see where they planned to set up the sawmill, but then decided against it and headed home. The quiet darkness of the woods met me as I climbed the ridge trail. I heard only the crunch of my own footsteps. Occasionally, I paused, turned on the light and scanned the woods with the piercing beam. Finally, I forced myself to concentrate on the path. When I got back to Botner's house Mom was already up making breakfast.

"Where were you?"

"I went for a walk. It's so quiet out this morning. Not too cold either." I sat down at the table.

John and I had breakfast and he left on the 267 trapline while I studied. I'd promised him if we caught anything I would skin it. Gay still slept. Mom mended for awhile then came back to the kitchen. I put my book down.

"Would it be okay if I went to visit Sandra when Gay goes?"

"No one is stopping you from visiting your sister." Mom kept wiping the countertop.

"I mean is it okay with you?"

"That's a decision you'll have to make on your own. It doesn't matter how I feel about it."

"In a way I'd like to see her. But then in another way…," I drifted off."

Gay came out of the bedroom and I resumed reading. She ate breakfast and joined me studying until John returned with a beaver in the sled.

"You didn't think we'd catch anything did you?" John picked the catch up by the base of the tail and carried it into the house. "You've got to skin it like you promised." He swung the catch up onto the table as Gay quickly cleared her books away. Glad for the break, I took out my pocket knife and started to work.

I'd made a slit in the fur and peeled away the soft belly covering before John went outside to chop wood and Mom and Gay decided to go down to the homestead to sort through clothes. We'd received packages on both north and south bound trains for quite some time after the fire. Now we had an overabundance of clothing in all sizes. It had become important for Mom to sort through them and send what we didn't need to others less fortunate.

When I flipped the beaver over onto its skinned belly and began working at removing the pelt from the sides and back, the door swung open. Ken entered, carrying an arm load of wood which he deposited in the box near the stove.

"I would have opened the door for you, but my hands were greasy, and Mom doesn't want me touching any door knobs or anything else when I'm like this."

"That's okay." Ken wiped sawdust off his arms.

"I see John caught you before you sneaked past the woodshed. There's fresh coffee if you want some." I motioned toward the stove, and resumed skinning. "But you'll have to serve yourself."

Ken took off his coat, threw it over a nearby chair and headed for the cups. He had a tall, lean look, and was about Bob's height, but he was older than Bob by several years. I tried picturing his face without the black beard and mustache. He turned from the stove with a full cup of coffee. I looked down and continued skinning.

I felt him watching me as he sipped on the coffee. Then he pulled a pocket knife from his jeans and opened it. "Let me help you with this thing. Then I'll go chop some alders and show you how to stretch it using a hoop."

We'd reached the tough muscle part along the back of the beaver where skinning became difficult. The hide, held securely to the carcass by muscle tissue extending up from the powerful scaled tail, needed to be skinned out slowly so as not to accidentally cut a hole in the most important part of the pelt.

"Have you ever been up to twin bridges at mile 270?" I asked.

"Sure, lots of times."

"Do you know about that cabin off the tracks at Mile 269 that is kind of nestled back into the ridge side?"

"I didn't think that old thing would still be standing. That was built years ago when there was a section house in the area."

"It's still standing. Needs some work though. I thought maybe I'd use that as a layover cabin. That way I could extend my trapline and hit the Indian River area. There's more game around there."

"When is all this going to happen?" Ken stopped skinning and took a sip of his coffee.

"Probably not until I'm out of school. Mom wouldn't let me do something like that until I was eighteen anyway. But then, with my own cabin five miles away from here I could have a dog team and run a circular line through the valley and along both the Indian and Susitna Rivers. That would bring me back home every other day."

"Sounds like you've done some scouting out of the area."

"I've been thinking about it for awhile." I kept skinning.

CHAPTER 25
The View

When Gay and I got off the train at Chulitna that Saturday, Doug and his large dog team waited. Huge snowflakes fell around us and we sunk up to our knees in the soft snowbank. We waited for the train to pull out and leave nothing but Gay, Doug, the dogs and me in silent surroundings.

"It's going to be hard going. I brought some snowshoes." Doug came over to us.

In a few minutes, he led off. The sled moved slowly through the fresh deep snow. The dogs panted as they struggled under their heavy winter coats to pull the sled around a lake and finally stop in front of a large log cabin.

Sandra stood in the doorway, a small child peering through her knees. "Hi Sis!" She waved. "Come on in out of that stuff. You both look soaked."

We shrugged out of our snowshoes and while Gay and Sandra talked I looked around. Sandra led us down a long hallway on one side of the house. There were two bedrooms and a bath off to the right. Then we broke through to a large front room which served as a living, dining and kitchen area.

"Too bad it's cloudy today. You can see Mt. McKinley through there on a clear day. The lake is down that way." She pointed out a picture window above the sink.

I took off my coat and sat in a kitchen chair. The counter area along a front wall below the string of windows was cluttered full of dirty dishes, open cans of food and garbage.

"Either of you want something to eat or drink?"

I shook my head and remained silent while Gay and Sandra talked about the cabin burning down and finally, Dave. Doug came in somewhere in between the conversation looking for dinner so Sandra and Gay started to cook. He remained fairly quiet during dinner, as did I. But the baby, which sat in a nearby high chair, threw and gurgled food, so I scooted my chair somewhat away from him.

"So what have you been doing, Meddy?" Sandra cleared the table and wiped down the child after he'd spread his food with his tiny pudgy hands all over his high chair.

"The same as always. School, trapline, helping out at the sawmill."

I looked down at the coffee ring on the table in front of me.

"Well." Doug stood. "I've got to get an early start on the trapline tomorrow, so if you don't mind, I'm going to bed." Doug disappeared down the hall and Sandra watched him.

"Tell me more about Dave." Sandra turned her attention to Gay.

I got up from the table to look out the window as far as lamplight allowed. The snow hadn't let up very much. I knew Doug would have a hard time on the trapline the next day.

"Where am I supposed to sleep?" I asked.

"You and Gay can sleep in the first bedroom. Take a lamp with you so you can see what you're doing."

I picked up a small kerosene lamp and took it into the bedroom, closing the door behind me. I could still hear Sandra and Gay talking as I sat on the sagging mattress and stripped off my clothes. Then I blew out the lamp and crawled under some blankets. The bed squeaked under me as I rolled over to lay with my eyes open in the dark. Dad had come home that weekend. I was missing his visit because of visiting Sandra. I wondered what Dad and Mom were talking about at that instant, where Ken was and if John had caught anything on the trapline. My thoughts settled on Ken and I was thinking of him when Sandra opened the door and held a lamp while Gay got ready for bed.

"Glad you came along?" Gay asked when Sandra left.

"I guess." I pulled the covers up around my neck and closed my eyes.

The same thoughts I fell asleep with awoke me that next morning. I peered out from under the covers to see Gay sitting on the edge of the bed, dressing. "I just heard Doug leave. Sandra's up too." She pulled a sweater over her head.

Sandra had a pot of coffee perking when I came into the kitchen several minutes behind Gay. After breakfast I helped Sandra with the dishes while Gay went outside to chop wood. I looked out across the lake. Snow still came steadily down. Behind me the child banged a spoon on the high chair's metal tray.

"You need more water?" Sandra came over to me with the teakettle.

"In a few minutes." I placed a dish on top of an already huge stack.

"It really means a lot to me that you came along this time." She put the kettle back on the stove.

"That's okay." I swirled some soap suds with my hand for a few seconds then continued washing.

"You're older, and you've changed, Sis." Sandra came next to me. "Maybe now you can understand why some of the things on the homestead happened like they did."

I watched the contents of the sink disappear down the drain, then turned to face her.

"All I know is that you ran off and married Doug as soon as you could get away. But before you did you made the homestead a living hell trying to get away sooner than Mom would let you."

Sandra stood in front of me. The sink was at my back, the stove to the right, and an L-shaped counter to my left. "Your turn is coming." She looked at me squarely. "And when it does you'll go after what is going to make you happy. No matter what's at stake."

"Well if I do, it won't be the way you did it." I turned, grabbed the teakettle off the stove and dumped its contents into the sink.

Gay came inside with a load of wood seconds later. "We'd better get an early start for the train this afternoon." She shook a layer of snow off her scarf. "That stuff is really deep and wet."

A half hour before train time, we prepared for the mile snowshoe trip to the tracks. Sandra stood in the doorway, child resting on her hip. "Come back and visit again soon."

"Okay." Gay stood up from buckling her shoes and I led off down the trail.

"Hey, wait up," Gay shouted.

"I don't want to miss the train," I shouted back to her.

"We've got plenty of time."

"I just don't want to take the chance."

CHAPTER 26
Go Away Little Girl

In the spring of 1965, and right before Easter, Mom went to town for a three week job as a live-in housekeeper. Because of that Gay had taken over the household operation. One spring morning she stopped kneading some bread dough on the kitchen table to watch me take another bucket of water into the bathroom.

"What are you doing?"

"I'm going to restretch that beaver hide and I need to soak it for a few hours to get it soft again."

"In the bathtub?"

"Where else can I do it? I'll clean up when I'm finished."

I took the hide, which we'd removed from the hoop quite some time ago, into the bathroom with me and pushed the stiff pelt down into the tub of water. The hoop had worked fine up until the time the hide started drying and pulled the flexible alders inward. The blanket-sized pelt had slipped back to a regular size. Since the time we'd made the hoop, John had discovered another piece of plywood and we'd been using it to stretch other hides that season. I was determined to get those few extra inches out of the pelt that I knew were there.

When I came from the bathroom Gay had just put her bread into loaf pans and worked at kneading a lump of sweet dough. She was preparing an extra treat for Dave who was coming up from Seward on that day's train to visit overnight. I sat down and watched. Gay wore a checkered shirt with sleeves rolled up to the elbows in wide, neat cuffs. She'd taken extra special care of her hair the night before. As I sat and watched her work, her hair glistened every now and then when it caught rays of sunlight streaming through the kitchen window.

I hadn't bothered to prepare for Dave's visit. My hair, straight and needing a shampoo, was tied back at the nape of my neck.

"I'm going to go study in the living room." I stood up.

Gay kept working with her specialty bread while I retreated to the couch with my text books. I heard someone enter the house a few minutes later and drop a load of wood in the box. Ken said something. Gay laughed, and I heard the door close.

"Where are Ken and John going?" I asked Gay after coming back to the kitchen to watch the men disappear down the trail to the section house.

"Cottonwood Island."

I watched until the forms disappeared then turned to Gay. "Do you think you could trim my hair again?" I looked at a handful of it. "I think the split ends are back."

Gay glanced at her wrist watch.

"We even have time to set it if we hurry."

I got the scissors and sat in a chair in the middle of the living room floor as Gay began the operation. She didn't have to cut as much off as before. Then I washed and dried my hair, put it in rollers and sat reading one of my textbooks near the heating grate in the floor.

Gay put her coffee cake in the oven and again looked at her watch. "The train is going to be here in an hour. You've got time to take a sponge bath. Then we'll unroll your hair."

When the train neared the station that afternoon Dave already stood on one of the several rung steps and hung onto the vertical bar of the baggage car. The train hadn't even stopped before he jumped off. He and Gay engaged in a long kiss. When they finally stopped, Dave turned around.

"Is that Melody? I didn't even recognize her." His eyes looked up and down. "I think I'll spend a little more time up here."

"Dave!" Gay slapped his arm playfully. "That's my little sister!"

I grinned and followed them as they started arm and arm up the trail to Botner's house. When we got there, Gay and Dave headed straight for the couch. I stayed at the dining room table waiting for Ken and John. But when I saw them coming up the trail, I hurried into the bathroom.

I heard them come inside a second later and stood behind the closed door listening to them talk. When Gay and Dave joined them in the kitchen, I combed my hair, opened the bathroom door and took several steps towards the kitchen.

Ken looked up. "What did you do to your hair?"

Gay answered before I had to. "We trimmed and set it."

"I liked it long."

"It's still long." She came over to me. "I think she looks cute, don't you?"

"I already thought she looked cute," Ken said.

My face was getting warm. I quickly scooped up my school books and headed for the living room.

"The couch is reserved." Dave grinned at me a few minutes later.

"Dave!" Gay slapped him playfully on the arm again.

"Well, it is."

"That's okay." I got up and went back to the kitchen. Ken was there alone, playing a game of solitaire. "What grade of school are you in?" he asked when I sat down at the other end of the table and opened a text.

"Tenth. I hope to make it into the eleventh by this fall."

"Are those courses pretty tough?"

"Not really. It's just hard to settle down to them sometimes and then when I do find a hard place, there's usually no one who can help me. So I just muddle through, hoping I'm doing everything right.

"Wouldn't going to school in Talkeetna be easier?"

"I guess. But I don't want to leave the homestead. Besides, I've come this far with correspondence school. And I've promised Mom and Dad."

"I quit school after the first half of the eleventh grade."

"Why?"

Ken shrugged. "Just didn't seem to be doing anything for me. I had no trouble getting part–time jobs even while I was in school. Then afterwards I went into the Army and learned everything I needed to know."

"But you were so close to graduating. Didn't you ever wish you'd finished?"

"No. It's just a piece of paper. You don't need it to get a job. In this country a person can get along fine without a high school diploma."

"But I don't know yet what I'll be doing. I just might need one. And I'm going to be on the homestead anyway, so I might as well study while I'm here. It sure can't hurt to have a diploma."

"I thought you were going to live out in the woods and trap."

"I am. But probably not all my life. I don't know what I want to do after that."

Ken shuffled the cards for a long time. Then he stood up and put on his coat. I looked up.

"Tell those two I said good night." He motioned with his head toward the living room, then paused. "And don't stare at me with those big brown cow eyes."

After he'd left I let myself break into an ear–to–ear grin.

CHAPTER 27
Springtime

Dave was supposed to leave that next afternoon but before he did, he and my sister continued to preoccupy themselves. I turned my attention to the soaking beaver pelt. After wringing it free of excess water, I brought the soaking hide into the kitchen and began tacking it to the board, careful to follow along the blanket sized outline I'd made with a crayon. The task took me most of the early afternoon to accomplish, but when I'd finally finished stretching the last inch possible out of the pelt, it measured to just blanket size.

Ken and John had come home for a quick lunch, saw Dave off on the southbound train, then returned to work. They were plowing a trail with the Cat from our new house up to Botner's. But the snow was deep and they'd been making slow progress. John showed up again way after dark to get a Coleman lantern, grab some sandwiches and leave. At 10 P.M., Gay was writing Dave a letter. I went out with a flashlight and a thermos of coffee to find the men.

I could hear the engine of the Cat as I walked the road to the section house and knew they were almost finished with the job. Since the original plowing back in January, we'd gotten several more feet of snowfall so the road looked as covered over as before. I walked the narrow path towards the oncoming Cat. Ken drove and John stood alongside in the deep snow with the lantern held high.

"You're not moving," John shouted.

Ken put the Cat in reverse, backed off a few feet, then tackled another bladeful of snow. When Ken saw me with the thermos, he shut down the piece of equipment.

"What's taking so long?" I asked.

"The tracks are slipping on the snow." Ken jumped down from the seat. He took the cup of steaming coffee I handed to him while John helped himself. "That's why I sent John back for the lantern. Sitting up here operating this thing with just the headlight isn't good enough. When I look down at the tracks and see they're moving, I think I am. But the Cat is really just sitting in one place treading snow."

I started laughing.

"It's not funny." John threw some grounds out of his cup and into the snow. "We're dead beat from fighting this thing all day. We probably won't get up to the house until midnight."

"I'm sorry. I just got this picture in my mind of Ken sitting on the Cat with this long white beard, and you alongside holding that lantern up high in one hand while leaning on a cane with the other."

Ken put his cup down on the track, grabbed me by the waist and threatened to dump me head first in the snow. John stood by, laughing.

"Stop." I could barely get the word out through my laughter. Ken had a firm hold around my waist with one arm. I was amazed when I couldn't free myself. I struggled against his strong closeness.

He let go. I fell backwards in the soft snow, then kicked him in the back of his knees. He buckled into the snow bank with me.

"Truce." I held my hands up.

Ken, already on his feet, took my arm and helped me out of the snow. Still laughing, I collected the thermos and cups while John got up on the spring seat of the Cat.

"I'm going to plow for awhile." He positioned himself.

"That's fine by me." Ken stood to the side.

"Do you want me to hang around and help?" I screwed the thermos cup back on.

Ken held the lantern as John started the engine.

"No. Go on back. There's not much you can do here."

The noise of the Cat made him shout the last few words. Then he wrapped his right arm around me, holding tighter than necessary for the guidance needed to help me onto the solid trail ahead of the Cat.

"See you in a little while." His eyes reflected dancing lantern light as he placed me safely on the trail.

I started home at a walk, but felt like taking high leaping strides. My body had stopped trembling by the time I got back to the house. Gay was already asleep. I waited in the kitchen and kept the coffee hot until the Cat finally crawled its way up the hill below the house. Then John killed its engine by the basement door.

"You want some coffee and pastry?" I asked when John came inside.

"You bet." My brother peeled out of his coat.

SPRINGTIME

"Where's Ken?" I asked.

"He went home. He was beat." John dove into the pastry, not even bothering to use his fork. "He said he'd be around tomorrow."

I waited for Ken to come over the next day. But he didn't show. We did get a message from Mom on the radio that she would be coming home on that night's train. I played solitaire with Ken's deck of cards, and waited.

"If you're going to the train you'd better get ready." Gay came out of the bathroom.

"Oh. Is it train time?" I looked at my watch. "You go ahead. I'll catch up." I started putting on my mukluks while Gay and John left with the flashlight.

I waited as long as I dared, then went outside the house and stood for a few minutes looking down the trail toward Ken's cabin. Gay and John had taken the only flashlight, but the moon shed just enough light to make walking by moonlight possible. I started out slowly.

Soon I heard the train. The noise of its far-away engine bounced off the surrounding mountains and came to me on quiet night air. Spring was on its way, but there was still enough chill to make me shiver.

"Kind of scary out here without a flashlight, isn't it?" Ken came up silently from behind and slipped an arm around my waist. I jumped and he held me firmly.

"You're spookier than a snowshoe hare that forgot to change color for spring."

"You startled me." I shivered again, but didn't feel cold.

We walked together silently. Ken kept his arm around me until we came in view of the section house.

"We didn't think you were going to make it." John was leaning against the front of the coal shed.

I didn't see Gay until Ken and I rounded the far end of the shed.

"It's chilly out isn't it? There's just enough breeze to go right through my coat." She put her hood up.

I leaned against the shed near her. Gay was between us. The three of us waited silently in the windbreak of the shed wall. When the train blew its whistle, she joined John who was out of view.

There was at least a minute before the prying light of the oncoming train disturbed the two of us.

155

CHAPTER 28
No More Land

    Sleeves rolled up past my elbows, I kneaded a mass of elastic bread dough on the kitchen table. Since Gay had left for her job on the train in late May, I'd been doing most of the cooking and baking. Especially when Mom was in town like that day. Downstairs, I could hear John and Ken working. Ken had become one of the family as far as my brother and I were concerned. He had even moved out of his old cabin by the creek to a small shed near Botner's house. He'd fixed it up with a stove, bunk and wash basin. When he wasn't building the house or teaching John how to weld, he pretty much stayed to himself and read westerns. I went to visit him every now and then. He always left the door open when I was there.
    I cleaned up the bread making utensils and looked out the kitchen window. From my vantage point above the basement, I saw John leave. He was going to check the river gauge, a job we started again in the spring when the ice went out. I knew he'd probably stop to visit with the state surveyors who had set up camp in their white tents alongside the tracks just opposite the section house. The surveyors were here to tie down the homestead boundaries in the area. This was the final step to receiving our patent to the homestead. John had kept close tabs on their progress.
    "C'mon down here," Ken hollered up the basement stairs. "I want to show you what we've been working on."
    I hurried down. Ken looked up from the work bench as I entered. My eyes adjusted to the dimmer light. "What is it?" I came up to the box–like frame made of welded ribar onto which Ken wrapped a blanket of chicken wire.
    "It's a fish trap." He stretched the wire and I watched. "This thing is heavy enough so you won't have to weight it down with rocks to keep the current from dragging it away." He tied off a piece of wire and snipped it free from the roll. Then he started the same cinching operation in another place several inches down.
    "Aren't there more fish at the mouth of the slough than in the river? I thought they came into the clear water to clean their gills."

"Maybe, but they don't stay long. They're all headed upstream. You have to catch them when they're running in the river."

"I'll bet you're wrong."

He looked at me and smiled. "It's a bet."

I watched Ken finish the trap. He'd shed his trapper's cap and mukluks for a black cowboy hat and boots which made him even more handsome. Ken looked up again and I felt caught.

"I've got to get this finished before John gets back so get yourself out of here." He smiled again.

"Okay. I'm going. I wasn't interested in your silly old fish trap anyway."

Once back upstairs I could hear Ken working. It seemed John would never return, but when he finally did, he brought news from the surveyors, which he shared with us at the dinner table.

"The surveyors say when they finish up here the State is going to make a blanket coverage of all unclaimed property." He scooped some vegetables onto his plate.

"You mean nobody will be able to homestead anymore?"

"Not unless they're twenty-one. And then it can only be a homesite. And only if it's land they open for entry."

"Twenty-one! That's too late. I don't want to wait until I'm twenty-one."

"Build a cabin and squat on the land. Nobody will care." Ken swallowed a forkful of food.

"It won't be the same. I wanted my own five acres. My own cabin."

"The surveyors said someone already staked that five acres you were after anyhow. A guy named Andrews filed just a few weeks ago. He's got a thirteen-year-old daughter, and is living there with her right now."

"Well I don't think it's fair. It always turns out that I'm too young to do what I want to do." I put my plate in the sink.

Ken came over next to me and gave me a nudge. "Let's go set that fish trap. The fresh air will do you good."

"Now? Won't we miss the train? Mom's getting off today."

"Naw. We've got plenty of time."

Actually, we barely had any time at all. Afterwards I left Ken and John at the building site and ran up the trail just as the train

157

pulled to a stop.

"Isn't Gay working on the train today?" I watched the dining car whisk past without seeing her usual wave.

"She quit her job."

"Why?"

"I guess she found a better one."

"She'll have to quit that one this fall too, won't she? In order to come back to the homestead and finish school?"

"She's going to go to school in town this fall, or maybe even leave the state."

"But she promised."

"Dad and I already figured she wouldn't be back." Mom paused. "That new girl and her father are walking down to visit today. I met him on the train when I went into town last week and I invited her to spend a few nights so you two could get to know each other."

We'd reached the house. I used my foot to push the front door open.

"Did John do any studying while I was gone?"

"No. But he and Ken did a bunch of work on the house."

"We're going to have this school thing out once and for all when Leon comes home the next time. How about you? Did you do any schoolwork?"

"Yes, I studied most of the time between making meals and stuff." I helped Mom unpack the groceries she'd brought home.

"Well, I just hope one of you stays here long enough to finish school like you all promised."

A knock on the door stopped the conversation. I opened it to see an older, slender man that could only have been Mr. Andrews. Standing alongside him was a girl I knew was two years younger than me, but she could have passed for Gay's age.

"Come on inside." I swung the door wide.

"This is Lenore." Mr. Andrews ushered the girl ahead. She was my height, with long wavy auburn hair. A sprinkle of freckles ran across her cute nose and highlighted a set of light brown eyes.

"Hi. I was just wondering…Do you have a bathroom scales?" She smiled.

I pointed the way and Lenore disappeared into the bathroom.

"Daddy," she came back into the kitchen with a pouting look. "You said with all the walking we did today, I'd lose weight."

"Maybe our scales weigh heavy," Mom suggested.

"Maybe." Lenore sat down and drummed her long polished and manicured fingernails on the kitchen table.

We looked at each other a few seconds. "Would you like to go see our homestead? We're building a new house."

"Okay." She popped up out of her seat. "You coming, Daddy?"

"No. I'm going to sit here and rest a bit, then head for home. You behave yourself while you're down here, young lady," he warned.

"Oh, Daddy." Lenore cuffed him playfully. "As if there were some trouble I could get into way out here in the boondocks."

Down at the building site, the first floor of the house had been framed in and the second story started.

"This place is going to be huge." Lenore walked through the open partitions on the bedrooms. I could hear Ken and John walking on the floor above us.

"We'll have three bedrooms, a bath, living and dining room, plus a separate kitchen." I showed it off. "This is going to be my bedroom over here." We walked between open studs to stand in a small rectangular area.

"You're lucky." Lenore looked around. "All we have is that leaky old cabin to live in."

"It took us a long time to get this far," I said. "C'mon, I'll show you the garden."

We walked the water trail, hopped the spring and then, after picking a few strawberries from the matted rows, started back to the house.

"Would you like to climb the mountain tomorrow?"

"Which one?"

"That one." I pointed to Disappointment.

"You've been up there? That's huge."

"We go up every summer. It's kind of a tradition. This time though I'd like to follow it all the way to the crest. I've only done that once before."

"I don't know."

"You'll lose some weight."

"Okay." Lenore nibbled the last of her berry.

John said he could climb to the top of the mountain in forty-five minutes. But I never liked to rush the trip. The next morning after two hours of steadily climbing along timber ridges and up a series of hogbacks, Lenore and I finally stood on top.

"This is really pretty. Where is the crest you were talking about?"

"Over there."

"Let's go then. I'm getting chilly."

We walked the deep rutted caribou path along the edge. I looked at the path ahead of me and on occasion glanced to my right for a panoramic view of the valley below.

"Hey, wait up," Lenore called out. "I want to get to the top the same time you do."

I found a large tundra boulder and sat on the layer of dried black lichen. Except for the surveyor's tents along the railbed, the valley looked the same as ever. But I knew the land wasn't free for settling anymore. Lenore sat down beside me, breathing hard.

"You see the section house?" I pointed.

"Yeah." She pulled her hair back behind her ears.

"Follow that straight back to our field then look slightly to the left. That shiny stuff is part of the roof of our new house. If you're real quiet, you can hear them hammering."

We sat still, listening to the small echoes. A gentle breeze rippled the shirt on my back. "Let's go." I stood. "If we sit here much longer we're going to stiffen up."

Lenore kept pace with me the remaining several hundred yards to the peak.

"Hey, what's that?" She pointed to a rock pile with a long piece of slate sticking out of the center.

"It's a monument I made the last time I was up here."

"I can't read what it says." Lenore bent down from the waist to study it.

I knelt and tilted my head. "I guess all the writing wore off. It was a long time ago."

"I'm going to make one of my own." Lenore began picking up rocks.

I walked to the edge and kicked a boulder down the stony face. It created a tiny avalanche before going into the shrubbery. Then all I could hear was the echo.

"Aren't you going to scratch your name in your monument again?" Lenore had finished her pile of rocks.

"Naw. It'll just wear off." I studied the valley. "Besides, I know what it's there for."

"I'm getting cold." Lenore rubbed her arms. "Can we go now?"

"Sure." We started back down the caribou worn path.

Maybe I wouldn't be able to stake my piece of land. But somehow I knew that wouldn't stop me from running my own dog team and trapping. I'd just have to use Gold Creek as a home base. And with more dogs, John and I could cover more territory. I had begun to work on the problem. By the time Lenore and I reached level ground that day, I had a firm plan in mind.

CHAPTER 29
When it Rains

There was just enough spitting rain that day on my way back from the Andrews' cabin to make the rails slippery, forcing me to walk the creosote ties. The calloused soles of my feet had been softened by the rain. It beaded up on the black timbers that stretched for miles between me and home. Normally, tie walking didn't bother me. But I preferred 'tight–rope' walking the rails in order to avoid the splinters, patches of sticky creosote, and grease that was always present on the ties. I looked down and chose my next footing carefully.

Lenore and I had started out early that morning, walking and talking the six miles to her Mile 269 cabin. I'd stayed to visit with her and Mr. Andrews until the south bound train went by. I'd been tempted to flag it down for the return ride. Sometimes the conductor would let us ride for free if it was just for a few miles. But, I always liked to be prepared to pay in case I had to. That afternoon I wasn't prepared, so I walked.

The rain came down harder, soaking my jacket. It trickled from my long hair down the sides of my neck. I lowered my head, turned up the collar of the jacket and stuffed my red cold hands into the pockets. The leather holster of the pistol allowed rain to track its way downward, soaking my leg. A raw spot began to develop where the soaking leg tie rubbed against bare skin with each step. I shivered and wished I hadn't worn shorts.

The trip to 269 took us two hours to walk that morning. Without Lenore, I had hoped for better time on the way back. But when I reached Indian River bridge at 267 and sought temporary shelter under its steel girdered structure, I realized it was going to be a slow return trip.

My stomach growled. I knew the family was probably eating dinner. Dad and Bob would be there too. It had been eight months since the fire. I pitched a rock into the swift current of the river then walked up to the bank and washed my dirt splattered calves and sore feet in the chilly water. They would be twice as dirty by the time I covered the remaining four miles if the rain kept up as it had been.

Bob's flashing smile came to mind then vanished when I heard the far–away sound of an approaching engine. I scrambled up the gravel embankment to the tracks and listened towards the north. I knew if I could get to a convenient place for the train to slow down, there was a chance they'd let me hop a ride. Hopping as fast as I could along the wet ties, I had reached a straight stretch in the tracks just as I recognized the pounding sound of the freight train as it crossed Indian River bridge. I stood to the side of the tracks and waited for the engine to round the bend. Freight trains didn't stop for passengers, but sometimes if the engineer recognized one of us kids and he was ahead of schedule, he'd give us a lift.

When the engine came into view I waved an arm and received the traditional two short blasts on the horn. Then as the train came closer, I held my arms bent at the elbow, palms up. I saw the engineer and raised my hands upward in two successive motions, then moved them back to the seat of my pants, slapping several times. A short blast on the horn told me my "lift up on the back end" message had been received and I stood waiting as the cars whipped past. The freight was long. I braced myself against the wind for some time before the cars began to slow and the caboose came into view. When it started past I latched onto the vertical grab bar and swung up onto the back vestibule.

"You're a long way from home on a day like this, aren't you?" One of the crew members shouted down to me from the crow's nest when I entered through the heavy metal door.

"I wasn't expecting the weather to close in. Thanks for the lift." I began climbing the runged ladder to the crow's nest.

"You headed down to Gold Creek or are you willing to give that God–forsaken place up and come with us all the way to the big city?"

"Just Gold Creek. I'm not ready for that big city stuff yet."

One of the other crew members relayed the message to the engine through a static ridden radio.

"You mean no young man has tried to whisk you away like your sisters?"

"Not yet." I sat down on the bench seat.

"Saw Dave at Chulitna," The brakeman continued. "He's got a nice cabin going up there. Right close to Sandy and Doug. Didn't see Gay though. Everything going okay between those two?"

"As far as I know. I don't keep track of stuff like that."

"I have the feeling they're headed for rough water."

"Why's that?"

"Age, for one thing. Sometimes it works out all right. But in this case I wouldn't bet on it."

"It seemed to work for Sandra and Doug."

"Maybe." The brakeman looked out the window for a second, then back at me. "But we see an awful lot from up here that no one else does." His eyes twinkled.

A message came over the radio from the engineer. The brakeman answered and put the receiver down.

"You don't mind being let off a bit north of the section house do you? The section crew is in and you are illegal cargo."

I nodded and climbed out of the crow's nest just as the caboose started over the Susitna River bridge. "Thanks again for the lift."

"No problem. Jump off the left side, okay?"

I waited for a flat place on the railbed before jumping. A few feet away, the cool mud of our Cat trail soothed my feet. The rain had stopped, but in its place a hoard of mosquitoes found and swarmed about me. I stepped up my pace, trying to outdistance them. As I approached the house, it appeared to be empty. I had hoped to have a chance to dry and comb my hair, change clothes and even wash my mud spattered legs again before seeing Bob. The mosquitoes redoubled their attack and I broke into a run just as the heavy kitchen door opened. Bob stepped out and I stopped short. I wiped my dripping hair back from my face and watched him, armed with his flashing white smile, approach.

"You're soaked," he laughed, then the look turned to concern. "Better change clothes before you catch a cold."

"I'm fine. I do this all the time." I wrung out my hair and walked with him the final few feet to the house.

Ken sat at the table and glanced up as we entered. "What happened to you? I've seen drowned cats look better."

"I got wet." I took a towel that Bob had retrieved from the bathroom and began drying my hair, then became immediately aware that Mom, Dad and John were talking in the living room.

"You missed dinner, but I think your Mom kept something warm in the oven." Bob took the towel when I'd finished.

"What's happening in there?" I unbuckled the cartridge belt and hung the weapon on its wall peg.

Ken shrugged, stood up, and went outside.

"Ken and I are going to get me settled in at his place," Bob said.

I stretched an arm up into a top cabinet, pulled out a plate, then rooted around in the silverware drawer to come up with a fork and knife.

"Tell your folks we'll be back soon." Bob still held the door knob. "Will you please change into something dry?"

"I'm okay."

Bob stood still, looking at me.

"After I finish eating, okay?"

"Fair enough." He flashed his smile and closed the door.

I put a forkful of food in my mouth and chewed as I watched the two men walk side by side down the road and out of view. Mom came into the kitchen.

"Are they gone?"

She saw me nod and went back to the living room. I didn't need to strain my ears to hear the continuing conversation.

"If it hadn't been for Ken and his influence you wouldn't be thinking about quitting school in the first place."

"I'm not thinking about it, Mom. I'm doing it," John said.

"I don't see why. If you plan to stay on the homestead anyway, you might just as well be studying. You said that yourself only last spring."

"But I'm learning more without studying at all. And I'm not going to do any more school work."

"We still have control over you until you're eighteen and you'll do what we say. I don't care how many Whitey Rudders or Kens influence you."

"That's ridiculous. Ken didn't influence Gay and she left."

"That's a different situation. If we have to we'll send you to town for schooling."

"Go ahead. It won't do you any good because I won't go to classes. You can send me to reform school if you want to. I don't care."

"Wait a minute, now," Dad's calmer voice interrupted. "Nobody's going to send you to reform school. There's no sense in threats."

165

on a patch of short green grass which grew in random tufts out of the blackened earth and after a few minutes decided I probably stood right where the heavy wooden table had been.

Turning from the area, I headed down the water trail to check the fish trap. My jeans soaked quickly from the morning dew on the field grass. The trap was empty. I resubmerged it in the swift current and watched the chicken wire disappear from view in the muddy swirling water. On my walk back, just short of our spring, I heard the unmistakable sound of lumber being piled.

"You're up and about early. Alice is wondering where you got off to." Ken was leaning against a stack of wood smoking a cigarette as I approached him a few minutes later.

"I couldn't sleep."

"Me neither. What's new about that?" He pulled another board from the stack.

"How much longer before the house is done?"

"A couple of weeks."

"You're going back to Talkeetna then?"

"I'd say I've about wore out my welcome here."

Ken threw the cigarette down and killed it with the toe of his boot. "Grab the other end of this stack and help me carry it to the house." He said without looking at me.

We were almost there with our load when Bob came out of the house and took my end of the lumber. "You should have called me. I was just in there not doing anything."

"I was managing." I stepped out of the way while they heaved the boards onto a growing stack near the house.

"You're soaking wet again." Bob turned back to me. "What are you trying to do? Catch pneumonia?"

"I can take care of myself."

"Your Mom said to send you home if we saw you."

I spun on my heel and started up the trail, passing Dad and John who were on their way to the new house.

"Where have you been?" Mom wanted to know when I entered.

"I checked the fish trap then stopped to talk to Bob and Ken at the house."

"You should leave a note or something when you take off like that so I know what's going on."

I grabbed a piece of cold toast off the table and poured myself a cup of coffee.

"You'd better get a note up to Lenore, too, so she'll be down today. I don't want you to have to be here alone while we're gone. And change those clothes before you catch a death of a cold," Mom said over her shoulder on the way to her bedroom to pack for the trip.

I scribbled a note to Lenore and got the letter to the section house in time for the north bound train, then stayed out of Mom's way the rest of the afternoon.

When the south bound train pulled up at the section house several hours later, Lenore hopped down the vestibule steps and watched the rest of my family board.

"What's up?" She wrinkled her brow.

"Mom, Dad and John had to go into town in kind of a hurry. I'm glad you could make it on such short notice."

"I wasn't doing anything up there but helping Daddy anyhow." She followed me across the tracks to the trail home. "What are we going to do here?"

"I thought maybe we'd go fishing at the mouth of Gold Creek. We could build a campfire and talk."

That night Ken joined Lenore and me. They built the fire while I fished. Then while I prepared the grayling we caught, Ken made a mesh of willow branches to roast the fish on. We'd just finished eating when Bob showed up. He'd taken the time to bathe, shave and change into clean clothes.

"If you want any fish you'll have to catch your own." I threw the last of the small bones into the flames.

Bob borrowed my pole and walked to the river's edge where Gold Creek's clear waters tumbled into the Susitna River.

"I'm stuffed." Lenore stood up. "I'm going for a walk. Anybody want to come?"

Ken was kneeling at the campfire, poking at the flames with a stick. "Sounds like a good idea to me." He stood up.

I begged out, and instead picked up the stick and continued to poke at the fire as the two of them strolled towards the bridge which was just a few hundred yards downstream. My attention focused on Bob. He made several casts, looked back at me, and reeled his line in.

"You sure you caught those fish out of there?" He leaned the pole against one of the log seats near the fire.

"You're trying too hard." I shoved some of the logs together with the stick as Lenore's playful scream echoed off the steel-girdered bridge.

Bob sat down next to me and watched me push at the wood. "So what are your plans?"

"What plans?"

"I mean what if John is going to be gone?"

"Nothing will change. If he does leave, he won't be gone forever. I'm going to stay here like I promised, finish my schooling and run my own dog team and trapline."

"Why?"

"Because I want to. Maybe I'll even build my own cabin."

"How are you planning to stake yourself?"

"I've got money from the bridge gauge job and strawberry picking. I'll be able to save enough in the next couple years to grubstake myself. If not, I'll sell some of the smaller furs."

"Those dogs are going to be pretty expensive to keep."

"I'll salvage train-killed moose in the winter and feed them salmon in the summer."

"Aren't you going to get lonely?"

"I don't need anybody. Besides, I don't plan to do it forever. Just until I prove to myself that I can do it."

We sat for a few minutes watching the sparks escape from the wood and drift upwards.

"I do the same thing, you know, with track at college. I like to prove to myself that I can run a certain distance in a certain amount of time. Then after awhile I don't have to prove it anymore, even to myself, and I can get on with doing something else."

The splashing sound of rocks and the mixture of Ken and Lenore's voices reached us. Bob stood up to get away from the smoke that insisted on drifting our way.

"I'm heading back. Let the others know for me, okay?"

I nodded, and closed my eyes from the smoke. When I opened them, he was gone.

CHAPTER 30
Caught

When Lenore went back home on the north bound train several days later, Mom, John and Gay got off.

"You just missed Bob," I said when we got back to the house and I watched my sister unpack the small overnight suitcase she'd brought with her.

"I know. Mom told me he was here for a few days. I guess John is going into the Job Corps or something. Did Mom tell you?"

"I haven't talked to her about it yet. How are you and Dave coming along?"

"Okay." Gay laid her nightgown on the bed.

"The railroad guys say he's got a nice cabin at Chulitna."

"It's beautiful."

"Are you two going to get married and live up there, like Sandra?"

"I don't know." Gay sat down on the edge of the bed. "Dave makes me mad sometimes. He wants to know why I can't be more like Sandra. I'm sure getting tired of people trying to make me into someone I'm not."

"You are going to school in Anchorage this year though, aren't you?"

"I don't have much choice. I know that unless I'm forced to finish school I never will. And I do want to finish. I just can't discipline myself to settle down to correspondence school." Gay played with a tuft of the bedspread pattern. "How are Mom and Dad taking John's ultimatum?" She looked up.

"I think John was kind of surprised they gave up the fight so easily."

"What are you going to do?"

"I'll hold the fort down until John gets back."

"If he comes back."

"He will. John loves this homestead too much to stay away any longer than absolutely necessary. It isn't as if he hates it like Sandra did."

"You don't have to hate it to not want to live here," Gay said.

171

"There is so much to explore in the city. When I start high school this fall, I can play in the band. And in the city there are other people... people who treat you like an adult." She looked at the bedspread.

"Let's go down to the new house," Gay said suddenly. "I haven't been here for a long time. It must be nearly done by now."

John and Ken were nailing on tin roofing when we got there. Gay walked inside.

"This is beautiful. I'll bet Mom's really happy. Look at all the windows." She stepped closer, pointing. "Real glass!"

We walked through the open front area of the house. I tried to explain how it was going to look when we'd finished with the inside.

"There's only three bedrooms? Where's mine?"

"I guess Mom and Dad figured you wouldn't be coming back to stay here for any length of time."

"They made one for John." Gay looked at the bedrooms again.

"You can bunk in with me when you come visit, or use John's room, he won't mind."

"That's okay." She peeled a small strip of bark off the edge of a rough cut wall stud. "What's up there?" Gay pointed to the ceiling.

I stepped into the hall and pulled a folding ladder downward. The ladder in its folded position blended in perfectly with the plywood ceiling. Only the cord I pulled downwards gave away its location. Once it was all the way down, we climbed up onto the second floor of the house. The large open room, its inside walls still unfinished, had more large windows.

"What are Mom and Dad going to do with all this space?"

"John and I are still going to be here. And I guess Mom intends to use this as a sewing room, library and study."

"It seems like an awful waste of time and money to build a place this big, now that both John and I are gone."

We listened to Ken and John above us as they walked and nailed the tin.

"Did Mom say when John would be leaving?" I asked.

"They don't know. She has to go to town one more time to sign some papers. Then John will have to wait until he's called. There has to be an opening in the school he applied for before he can go. It could be a few weeks, or months."

Boy and another collie–husky–shepherd mix from Mr. Andrews. He'd brought two pups to his place in early winter. By spring he'd given me one that refused to pull a sled. Mr. Andrews had named him Whimpy.

I knew by the size of Whimpy's paws and his long rangy legs that he'd be a big dog by the next trapping season. With Spook and Papeete to help me train, there would be no trouble breaking him to harness. Boy, though, was a different story. The animal was given away because of his uneven temperament. Boy responded to the sight of a harness with a mixture of snapping, whining and snarling. Whether he'd gotten his fears through cruel training or some other fashion, I knew it would take most of that summer to win him over.

I'd already started his training by sitting near him while he ate. Then I'd left a harness in his view hanging from the bough of a nearby spruce tree. My final play was to let him wear the harness for small periods of time.

My schoolwork had slipped the past winter. The lengthened trapline and increased burdens of taking care of the homestead had set me behind schedule. Although it was true that there were only two people to take care of, the jobs didn't disappear proportionally. We had still used as much wood over winter keeping the house warm. Shoveling snow off roofs took four times as long. Even the trapline had taken more time because John wasn't there to help. But I knew if I could knuckle down to my courses that summer I still stood a decent chance of getting into my senior year of high school by the fall.

Spring had started out perfect. Without the usual spring rains Mom and I were able to work late each night painting the house. By June the field was dry enough to till and plant. It was my goal to get the job completed before the middle of the month, so that way we would have a good crop of grass, part of which could be scythed by hand and dried as bedding for the dogs.

That meant building some kind of shed to store the bedding in, and one afternoon as I maneuvered the Cat into ever tighter circles with the disc following behind, I thought about that next chore. When I'd finished discing for the day, I drove the Cat back to the garden where I was surprised to see Lenore standing by the strawberry patch. She came running over after I'd killed the engine.

177

"Daddy had to go to town and he said the house would be all right by itself now that things aren't freezing anymore. So I came down here."

"Good. We can study together again."

"I didn't bring my school books."

"Why not?" I hopped off the spring seat.

"There's a new state program that lets kids in the bush go to school in the city without costing the parents anything. Did you know that?"

I looked at her and raised my eyebrows.

"No kidding. It's a kind of deal where I'd live with a foster family for the school year. The state pays the family to provide for me and I even get a spending allowance for clothes and stuff."

"Does your Dad know about it?"

"Daddy? No. I'm going to fill out some forms that the state sent. Then by this fall when all the arrangements are made I'll let Daddy know."

"Do you think he'll mind you doing that?"

"No. He already told me that if I could figure out a different way to get my high school education that I was welcome to do it."

The next few days Lenore followed me around and helped with chores while we talked about the possibility of her going to the city. She talked about dancing, boys, cars, and a few things that I'd never done before. The last time I'd seen a movie in a theatre was before we'd left San Francisco six years ago. And I'd never been to a dance. Lenore had showed me a few dance steps the previous winter when I spent time with her at her cabin. We'd even shaved our legs once and put on a pair of nylons, then sat at the table swapping boy stories. Lenore had more to swap than I did.

When she got on the train headed for home a few days later, Dad got off. He hadn't made it home very often after John had left. And when he did, I usually dropped all my chores. But I'd already started digging a cesspool for the house and was anxious to finish it. A few hours after Dad's arrival, I came inside the house and flopped down in a kitchen chair. Mom and Dad were already sitting at the table.

"I just can't dig that thing any deeper. The rocks are getting too big."

"How deep is it now?" Mom asked.

"Not even five feet."

"Let it wait. When I get some time off work I'll dig it out." Dad put his coffee cup down.

"Okay. Tomorrow I'll do some more discing."

"Let that go too," Dad said.

"But it has to be done."

"John can take care of it next spring when he gets home."

"Okay. I'll help Mom weed the strawberry patch again and take care of the garden. The potatoes need to be hilled."

"How about doing some schoolwork?" Dad said.

"I can do that when it rains."

"And what if it doesn't rain? Are you going to just keep putting it off?"

"She hasn't touched a schoolbook for over two weeks." Mom stood up and removed some empty coffee cups from the table.

"I'll catch up."

"It's that trapline that put you so far behind this past year. If you had been studying during the winter, you'd be free to enjoy the good weather and not worry about schoolwork."

"I can't study all the time during the winter. Besides, the trapline is important to me."

"There just might not be any trapline this next winter unless you catch up with your studies."

"All I need is one more year to get enough wolverine and beaver for the parkas."

"Then you'd better decide how important that is to you and start knuckling down to those schoolbooks."

"But there's so much to be done right now."

"And you could have the time to do it right now if you'd studied over the winter."

"I did study. I'm not any farther behind than I was a year ago. Give me credit for holding my own, anyhow."

"Well, I think it's pretty obvious that before long you'll be eighteen and still in school."

"I said I'd finish before I'm eighteen and I'd do it right here. What else do you want from me!"

"We'll see."

I stormed to my bedroom, pulled my textbooks off the shelf and threw them on the bed.

Hours later I still sat on the bed and had chewed off the eraser of my pencil. When Mom and Dad went to bed early, I stayed up to study. I was up again early the next morning before either of them pounding away at a typing and an American History lesson. I wanted to have both of them ready for the train that afternoon. When I went to the section house with my lessons there was a note in the mailbox saying someone named Alice Powell in Talkeetna wanted to talk to me right away. A phone number had been scribbled below the message. I stared at the piece of paper and remembered Ken had talked about Alice Powell. She owned the Talkeetna Motel.

My hands were sweaty when I used the section house phone to dial the number. It rang three times before someone answered.

"Talkeetna Motel." A voice chimed.

My mouth went dry. I heard my heart in my throat.

"Is anybody there?" The voice queried.

"Yes. It's me. Melody Erickson. I got a call…"

"Just a minute."

I held the receiver in the crook of my neck and wiped my hands on my jeans.

"Hello, Melody dear?" A voice crackled over the line.

"Yes."

"Someone told me you might be interested in coming to school in Talkeetna this fall. I want to offer you room and board plus wages for the work you do for me here at the motel. We would arrange your working hours around the time you'd need to go to school and do homework."

"I. . .I don't know."

"Well, you think about it, honey, and give me a call back tomorrow."

"Okay. Sure." I held the phone tight.

"I hope you decide to come down, dear. You talk it over with your folks and let me know." The receiver on the other end clicked.

I held onto the phone a few seconds then hung up. The farther I got down the trail the more excited I got about the call. By going to school in Talkeetna that fall I'd still be close enough to the homestead to come up and visit. And it wouldn't cost Mom and Dad anything.

"It isn't the money," Mom said when I told both of my parents the next day about the call. "We could afford to support you if you wanted to go to a public school. I thought you wanted to complete correspondence school."

"I did. But there's so much to do out here besides schoolwork. I just can't turn my back on all of it. Every time I try to get something done it seems like two jobs replace the one I just finished. At least in Talkeetna I'd have regular work and school hours."

"You could work out regular school hours here," Dad said.

"I just think I'd have more free time, that's all."

"How? You'll be working at the motel during all of your free time. I'd think you would have learned from Gay how difficult it is to work and go to school at the same time."

"I just want to get out of high school before I'm eighteen, like I promised."

"You aren't going to do that by going to Talkeetna or any other public school. You're not out of the eleventh grade yet. That means they'll start you off in the eleventh grade down there this fall. Instead of being just a half year behind, you'll end up a full year behind."

"And what about your trapline?" Mom said. "Don't you still want to run one this winter?"

"I didn't think you and Dad were going to let me run one anyhow."

"I have no quarrel with the trapline as long as your studying gets done."

"I feel like I'm fighting a losing battle out here. Everything is growing up with weeds and needs tending to faster than I can get to it. My schoolwork is getting behind and even you don't think I'm going to finish school up here." I grabbed a tissue. "Well, maybe you've been right all along. Maybe I can't do it." I didn't even bother to stop the tears I knew were on their way.

"But you are so close," Mom whispered. "You're the only one in the family that has made it this far. And you had such firm plans. I just don't understand why this sudden change of heart."

"I'm tired, okay?" I blurted. "I'm tired of being told what I can't do instead of what I can do. I'm tired of being compared to everybody else." I had tried not to glare but knew from the look on Dad's face it probably hadn't worked. I lowered my eyes and sat sobbing. Finally Dad came over to the couch and sat next to me.

"I know I've been tough on you. Maybe I've been too tough. But going to Talkeetna is not the answer. If you feel you have too many chores and they keep you from doing your school work, I accept that. Mom and I will do everything we can to help make it easier. We need to work this whole thing out together."

"I'm just not sure of anything anymore. Nobody else has made it. What makes me think I can? Even Lenore is leaving."

"You can do it, Melody," Dad said softly as Mom gave me another tissue.

They stayed for awhile then left me alone in the house. I pulled the tissue in little pieces and sat crying for a long time before admitting to myself that Dad was right. I wouldn't be saving any time by going to Talkeetna. But something in me still wanted so desperately to leave – something I could only cry about. I finally dried my eyes and headed back to the section house.

CHAPTER 32
A Different Breed

"Mom?" I fastened the tie on my holster around my right leg while speaking softly to a mound under the rumpled bedcovers. "It's almost 8:30. I'm going now. I made some fresh coffee cake last night."

She pulled the covers away from her face. "Okay. You go ahead. I'm awake."

Outside, a shadowy morning dawn lingered. The akhio creaked as I fastened the tow lines. The dogs whined anxiously. In minutes I had all four in the traces. Spook leapt at the command and the sled swished over an early March snow trail. We'd be across the bridge by daybreak.

I'd been taking care of Mr. Andrews' cabin off and on the whole winter when he went into town. That day, after checking my trapline, I would travel the extra mile to his cabin, spend two days alone there and keep the fire going so things wouldn't freeze up.

I hopped out of the akhio as Spook began climbing the snow-covered wooden stairs that led up to the threshold of the bridge. When the team reached the tracks, I checked to make sure their traces weren't tangled then put my parka hood down. There was no sound of a train in the cold morning silence. I stepped back into the akhio and sent Spook ahead onto the bridge ties.

Enough snow clung to the ties to make the sled pull easily so I rode instead of running alongside. Still, I urged all four dogs into a fast trot. They were arranged in a four dog hitch that kept Spook in the lead, Papeete behind in single file, and the two youngest, biggest dogs closest to the akhio in tandem wheel position. This way Spook didn't have to pull at all anymore. Papeete, because of his pint size, and inability to get along with either of the other two dogs, also ran by himself. He held his tail high and had his hackles raised in defense of his position. Whimpy, the largest of the dogs, except for Spook, had become an eager puller, always leaping into the traces. But Boy, after I'd spent hours of separate training with him, still just did the job required without showing any of the spirit the other dogs possessed.

When we reached the end of the bridge, the dogs picked up the pace as the akhio slid onto the hard packed surface between the rails.

They had caught a scent and lengthened their lope. I held on tight, still standing in the akhio. Several large shapes some distance down the tracks came into view. Moose traditionally followed the packed railbed as a relief from the deep snow in the woods. They stepped up their long-legged trot as the dogs began a full pursuit. I let them have their head until they closed the gap to several hundred feet, then hauled back with all my weight on the trace line and shouted for Spook to slow the pace. The big dog hauled up eagerly, sides heaving. Seconds later both moose broke for the woods.

"Okay, fellas. Party's over. Let's go." I made a clicking noise with my tongue that brought the dogs back to the job at hand.

In another mile Spook left the tracks to follow the trapline trail down into the 265 swamp. He automatically stopped at every set. But I'd learned long ago to watch Papeete. He always gave me advance notice if I'd caught something. Three sets into the swamp, he sniffed into the air and his tail swung wildly from side to side. I stopped the team and walked the few paces to a small animal set under the bank of a swamp stream. Papeete whined.

A few minutes later I remade the set and dropped the catch into a gunny sack in the sled. A half-mile later we had added a cross fox. Then, before exiting the swamp to follow the frozen snow covered blanket of river ice upstream to Indian River bridge, Papeete's hackles stood on end.

I stopped the akhio, tied the sled with the drag rope to a nearby tree, then approached the wolverine set cautiously.

The dry spruce drag pole I'd fastened a #4 trap to was gone. Torn ground around the base of a spruce tree that still held a large chunk of rotten salmon told me the trap had a good hold on the prey. I unsnapped the leather holster catch that stretched over the hammer of the pistol and looked back towards the dogs. They sat uncommonly quiet. Papeete, ears up, sat at attention and sniffed the wind.

The set had been made at the base of a ridge where it met the swamp. Like most of my wolverine sets, I'd placed the trap and bait near a beaver house. I examined the tracks that waddled over the top of the house to the demolished circle. I knew he was there somewhere. Somewhere close. I smelled his rage.

There were no drag marks leading away from the set, so I walked a few feet farther up the trail, squatting down occasionally to look at intermittent gouge marks in its hard-packed surface. The wolverine had pulled the pole behind him vertically instead of horizontally and hadn't created the drag needed to stop him. I stood up and studied the trail far ahead, then focused on what I searched for.

The break in the ice on the swamp's edge was small. Minutes later, I approached it cautiously, careful to keep away from the weakened sides of the freshly caved-in dry pocket. The pockets along the edges of beaver swamps were common by this time of year. Water volume had decreased throughout the winter and receded from the edges, leaving an ice bridge over the empty swamp floor. It was along such an edge the wolverine had dug his way underneath. The closer I got, the more I recognized the furious grunts as the wolverine struggled against the drag pole which had wedged itself on a ragged edge of ice above the cave in.

I stood well back from the hole, trying to decide which direction under the ice the wolverine hid. A light pull on the pole from a respectable distance confirmed my suspicions. The next time I pulled at the pole, I was holding the cocked and ready .22 in my left hand.

The large clawed, captured front paw came forward first, then a froth-covered, white-fanged head. With black gums pulled back to issue a bone-chilling growl, the wolverine feigned attack. I released the pole and he moved back under cover, snarling warnings. I held my hand steady the next time, anticipated his reaction and fired without aiming. The resistance stopped. Still leveling the pistol at the hole, I pulled out a limp quarry, nudged it with my booted foot, then holstered the pistol. Only then did the chill work its way through my body.

Minutes later, with the wolverine hefted over my shoulders, I dragged the pole and trap back to the set. I had five wolverine. Five would be enough for a parka. Six would have been better. I dumped the animal in the sled, looked at it, then threw the unset trap into the sled too and gladly settled for five.

We came up onto the tracks at Indian River without any more excitement and I headed the dogs north. The team arrived at Mr. Andrews' cabin as dusk settled. I built a fire in the stove then unhitched and tied up the team. The balance of the day was spent skinning out my catch. Although Mr. Andrews had a limited number of stretching boards himself, neither the fox or wolverine pelt would have dried in the few days I had at the cabin, so instead, I stretched only the marten hide, rolled up and placed the other two pelts in the gunny sack and hung it off a nail protruding from the gable outside the cabin. They'd freeze and I'd stretch them on my own boards when I got home.

With the dogs finally fed, I sliced some meat off a hunk of moose tenderloin that Mr. Andrews had brought in from his larder and placed on the counter to thaw. I slapped the steaks into a smoking skillet and turned them with a fork. In a few minutes, I sat at the table eating when a movement caught my eye. I sat still and waited for the little white head to poke through a small hole by the kitchen door.

"C'mon in," I invited. "Nobody's going to hurt you."

When the visitor didn't return, I continued eating. I'd never met Mr. Andrews' 'pet' whom he fondly called Willy the Weasel. Weasels were good mousers, and that was an excellent reason to make friends with one. Mr. Andrews told me that Willy had become so tame that often he'd wake up in the mornings to the little animal's scoldings, open his eyes and see the feisty critter standing on top the sleeping bag.

But Willy hesitated to enter the cabin in my presence so I finished my meal, washed the dinner plate and took the lamp into the living area. I pulled some books out of another gunny sack I'd brought up in the sled with me, unwrapped the protective plastic and lay down on the bed.

At home, Mom and I had worked out a system to provide me with the most school hours possible. My days started at about midnight when she awakened me to take my turn at keeping the range and furnace fires going. I'd get up, get dressed and settle down in front of the kerosene lamp to study. At about seven or eight, Mom would usually wake up on her own and make breakfast. That was my cue to put my books away and start the day's chores. After chores and breakfast, I'd get ready to go on the trapline. I always started out before daybreak and usually got home before dark which, in the grip of winter, was somewhere around three in the afternoon. Mom always had the dogs' dinners ready. After their dinner, and ours, I'd chain them up then head straight for bed.

Our routine had worked out well and we'd stuck to it even over the holidays when John came back on Christmas leave from the Job Corps. He'd run the trapline with me several times and helped me skin the game like we'd done in years past. It was then I'd revealed to him as well as Mom and Dad, my thoughts about going to college the following fall to study veterinary medicine. I'd already been in touch with the assistant superintendent of schools for our district to see if I could join a graduating class in the city that next May. I promised to finish my high school correspondence classes by the following fall. I had figured John would be home that next April, and with him there to help out with the summer chores, I'd have plenty of time to finish my high school courses by that time.

A clunking sound in the kitchen alerted me. I got up off the bed quietly and brought the lamp with me. The moose tenderloin was gone from the counter. I followed the bloody trail across the plywood floor where the piece of meat blocked the small hole near the kitchen door. The meat moved in little sporadic jerks.

"You can't pull that piece of meat through that tiny hole." I bent down and tugged. The resistance stopped immediately. I picked up the meat, brought it back to the counter and trimmed away dirt it had collected on its journey. Then, wrapping the remaining tenderloin in some foil, I stored it in a cool place under the sink. The scraps were dropped at the front of the hole.

Willy was nowhere in sight, but I wasn't surprised when the scraps disappeared overnight. The tiny footprints in a half-inch of fresh snowfall told on the visitor.

CHAPTER 33
John Returns

Mr. Vondalee S. Page   April 15, 1967
Assistant Superintendent of Schools
Palmer, Alaska

Dear Mr. Page:

I would be most anxious to join the graduating senior class at Wasilla High School this spring and as you have advised, I will try to finish as many of my courses before that time. However, I do anticipate not being able to finish two of my twelfth grade electives by June 1st. But I promise you that after graduation I will continue my studies and complete these courses before September when I hope to be admitted to the University of Alaska.

As for the diploma itself, since the University of Nebraska Extension Division does not issue any diplomas, I would rather have one from Wasilla High School than a G.E.D. from the State of Alaska. I hope arrangements can be made for this.

I will keep in touch with you about my progress, and hope to meet you in Wasilla to offer my personal thanks to you for all the help you've given me these past several years.

Sincerely,

I reread the contents of the letter while it was still in my typewriter, trying to decide whether it needed a sixth recomposing. Then I pulled the sheet of paper from the smaller portable machine Mom and Dad had given me the past November on my seventeenth birthday and applied a neat, controlled signature to the bottom of the page. I folded the letter and slipped it into a previously addressed and stamped envelope.

"You'd better hurry. It's almost train time." Mom looked at her watch.

Outside, a light sprinkle of snow over the crusted white surface squeaked underfoot like powdered sugar and carried the message of my presence as I headed up the section house trail. That special freshness had come back to the air once again. I had anxiously witnessed the familiar white veil draw back to expose a new spring.

I heard the passenger train as it approached the Susitna River Bridge and began to run. The train had already rounded the bend when I reached the section house. With no time to look for the mail hoop I stood by the side of the tracks and held my hand high as the engine passed. The train slowed slightly. A baggageman peered out from behind the huge double doors of an approaching car. He reached out and grabbed the letter. I stood back and watched the rest of the yellow and blue coach cars whip by.

Once home, I put away the typewriter then retreated to my bedroom and pulled back the cloth curtain covering the small closet to reveal three dresses Mom had bought the last time she was in town. I selected the one I planned to wear under my cap and gown on graduation night and laid it on the bed. A few minutes later I stood in front of the full length mirror in my bedroom wearing the sleeveless robin egg blue dress. Two strips of delicate lace, about 12 inches apart, ran from the collarless neckline to the hem. I looked down at my lumberjack–stockinged feet and wiggled my toes.

"Mom?" I shouted up the hallway. "What am I going to wear for shoes at graduation?"

"I guess you're going to need some heels. Why don't you look through the Sears catalog and find a style you like. Clip the picture out and send it into Madge. She can have John buy them when he comes through Anchorage on his way home next week."

"What about this?" I came into the kitchen with the open catalog several minutes later.

"Those look terribly high. Try to find something shorter. You don't want to be taller than the boys."

I flipped the pages. "This is exactly what I want." I grabbed the scissors.

Mom looked over my shoulder as I cut. "Those are nice. Be sure you write John a note and tell him you want them simple, like in the picture, with an average heel and in white. You'd better enclose a tracing of your foot."

I mailed the letter on the next train and waited two of the longest weeks before John finally arrived home. We exchanged bear hugs and I snatched the obvious shoe box from under his arm. I carried only the small box while Dad pulled a sled load of John's belongings behind me and my brother struggled under a large duffle.

"When I saw the size you were going to need," John watched me untie the package when we got home, "I just told the clerk to keep the shoes and fix me up with a couple of boxes."

"Mom!" I complained.

"John, stop teasing her."

"Actually, I couldn't find anyone to wait on me at the store so I just took the picture and instructions and chose them all by myself."

I pulled the lid off, pushed the protective tissue back and picked up one of the shoes. "They're perfect."

"Of course they are. I might not be good at algebra, but I can match up pictures with the best of them." John grinned.

"Put a pair of my nylons on your feet before you slip into those." Mom said as I retreated down the hall to my bedroom. "They'll fit better."

I found the nylons, put the shoe box on my bed and sat down next to it. In a few minutes I was back.

"You walk like you're wearing snowshoes." Mom shook her head. "Take smaller steps."

I did, then turned and lost my balance.

"You know what they say about taking the country out of the boy." Dad said. "I guess it holds true for girls, too."

"Wait until she puts a dress on. That'll keep her from taking large steps." John suggested.

"I just need practice." I stood on one foot, pulled off the left shoe and looked into it.

"Do they hurt?" Mom asked.

"A little."

"You need to break them in is all. But be careful not to get them smudged."

"I'm going to take them off now." I removed the other shoe and walked back down the hall. The nylons had slipped down to bulge around my ankles.

"Why don't you and John go up and get the mail?" Dad suggested when I came back.

John waited for me to get my boots on, then we headed for the section house where I recovered several graded lessons. I ripped open the envelopes to read my grades.

"How much more do you have to go before you're finished?" he asked as we started the trail back home.

"All I have to finish up before graduation is my shorthand class. The other two courses I'm finished with. But I can't send the lessons in too fast in case I've goofed something up. It takes so long sometimes to get lessons back. But I've learned it's better to wait for the graded lessons before sending the next ones in.

"I'm sure glad you're back," I continued. "We were so busy getting in wood last year and finishing up the house that I didn't get to work the field. We're going to need wood again for the coming winter too. And Dad plans to finish the cesspool as well as put a telephone in for Mom."

"I'll do what I can. But I'm not going to be here for long, or over the winter."

I stopped walking. "What do you mean? We talked this over last Christmas about how I'd be going to college this year while you stayed on the homestead with Mom."

"I joined the Navy. I have to report for induction two weeks from now in Anchorage."

"You won't even be here for my graduation?"

He shook his head.

"Of all the dumb things to do. How could you? Now of all times."

John held my glare. "I didn't have much choice. It's either enlist now or get drafted on my nineteenth birthday. This way I at least got to choose the area I wanted to go into. If I waited until they drafted me I'd end up in the infantry and in Viet Nam."

"How long will you be gone?"

John shifted his eyes. "Six years."

"Six years! I can't stay on the homestead with Mom another six years."

"You could start your college education through correspondence. Dad said that the University of Alaska accepts a certain number of correspondence credits towards a degree."

"No way. I'm just finishing up seven years, summer and winter, of correspondence school. And I'm not going to wait any longer than this fall to go to college either."

"Nobody said you had to."

"What did Mom and Dad say about your enlistment?"

"Mom doesn't know. Dad's probably telling her right now. She'll take it the same way you did. But when Mom sees I had no other choice, she'll understand."

When we arrived back home, Dad was outside chopping wood. I went to my bedroom to file my lessons.

"I want both of you to be there when I go in for induction," John was saying to Mom when I came back to the living room.

"C'mon upstairs," I said to John. "I've got something to show you."

My brother waited while I pulled down the folding ladder. Once upstairs, I stood on top of a large chest of drawers, removed a piece of plywood that gave me access to the attic, and began pulling down the pile of stored furs.

"How many more are up there?" John's arms were full.

"You don't even have a third of them yet." I began pulling down the beaver and wolverine pelts.

"You must have had a pretty good year." He dropped his armful to receive more.

"Remember this one?" I handed a stiff pelt downwards.

"Our first." John turned the hide over and over. "I'll never forget him. Caught in your #3 on the day Mr. Ihly died."

"And this one?" I dropped an oblong stretched beaver pelt downwards.

"You've still got this ratty old thing?" He loosened the twine and unrolled the hide. We stared at it for a long time.

"Think we've got enough for parkas?"

"Only one wolverine parka. That will be for Dad. You're going to have to be satisfied with a beaver parka like the rest of us."

"When are they going to be made?"

"I don't know. But they will be. Until then, the furs will keep nice and safe right up here."

John helped me store the furs away and I slipped the attic panel back in place.

"You two come down now," Mom shouted. "Dinner's ready, and then Melody has to study. I don't want her slipping behind."

"Mom and Dad have aged." John said as he helped me down from the dresser.

"Really? I hadn't noticed."

"You will." We walked slowly to the stairs. "Ever hear from Sandra?"

"She's getting a divorce."

"What about Gay?"

"She went to New York. But she'll be back. I know she will."

"John." I stopped. "You'll write to me, won't you? I mean, more than you wrote in the past."

"Sure. I'll write."

With that promise and John's playful help those next few weeks while I practiced walking in the new shoes, I kept myself from thinking about his departure. When the day finally came we gave each other our bear hugs. Then he took a step back to look at me as Mom and Dad boarded.

"Don't go embarrassing me by walking like a homesteader when you accept that diploma." He put on his best Whitey Rudder face. "Guess when I see you again, you'll pert' near be a college idiot."

He turned and dashed up the vestibule steps two at a time.

The house seemed strangely quiet when I returned. I walked through John's bedroom. He'd not even had a chance to decorate it. Mom and Dad already planned to tear out the bedroom partitions so more room could be added to the living area. My room looked the same as it had the year before, except for the dresses that hung in the closet and the white high heels, still wrapped in tissue paper in their box on my dresser. I picked up the box, sat on the edge of my bed and slipped into the shoes with my bare feet. Mom had been right. They didn't fit too well that way. I pulled the heels off, let them drop to the bearskin rug, and lay back on the bed. The tears came first, then uncontrollable sobs. I pulled a pillow over my face.

In a few minutes it was over as quickly as it had started. I sat back up, wiped my eyes and opened a book to the few final lessons.

CHAPTER 34
"Always Forwards, Never Backwards"

"Does it fit okay? We weren't sure what size hat you'd wear. It looks like it might be a bit small. Here let me put some bobby pins in, just to make sure."

I sat down on a long bench while she operated.

"We didn't know you were coming until this year's tassels had already been ordered, so you don't have one you can keep. Luckily one of the students ordered an extra one for his mother. He brought it along so you could use it in the ceremony."

"That's fine." I nodded.

A few minutes later the lady returned and attached the red tassel, dropping it over the edge of my cap.

"Everybody please line up in rehearsed order," she spoke loudly. "Melody, you're fourth in line. I'm so sorry you couldn't make it for rehearsal. But you'll be fine. Just follow what the other students do. It's a short and simple ceremony."

I took my place and wished there were a few more students in front for me to watch before I would be called upon to receive my diploma.

"Your attention, students." The lady passed out pieces of paper as she walked from the head of the line.

The front cover had a picture of a white cap. A spray of red and pink roses separated it from a rolled up diploma tied with a deep pink ribbon.

"These are your programs. Look through them quickly. There's nothing here that you weren't told about in the rehearsal."

I opened the single 8 x10 page. On the left hand side was the heading "Class of 1967." I searched for and found my name. It had a small asterisk beside it. I quickly followed the annotation to the bottom where it explained "Correspondence student from Gold Creek."

Below the double column of names was the class motto: "Always Forward, Never Backward."

I skipped the usher section and quickly read the commencement program on the right hand side of the page as we started a rapid walk through the halls. We halted suddenly to one side of the gymnasium door.

The group stood in silence under the watchful eye of the lady. I shifted my weight from one foot to the other. When the music started I could hear my heart. Suddenly we were under the bright lights of the gym. I looked up and tried to find Mom and Dad in the crowd of people who stood on either side of our progressing line.

Not seeing either of them, I looked back down, aware that I'd lost the step we were supposed to use to *Pomp and Circumstance*. I spent only a few seconds trying to fake the step and again looked up. This time I spotted Dad, who wore a suit. Mom was wearing a dress. A glimmer came into his eyes before he said something to Mom.

We'd begun the left hand turn in front of the first row of folding chairs. When I reached mine I remembered to remain standing. Then I looked to my right. There was a huge gap between me and the student who was supposed to be standing right next to me by now. I felt myself blushing with the realization that I'd hurried too fast to get to my seat.

"Sorry," I whispered, when she and the rest of the line caught up with me.

We continued standing through the invocation, during which I took turns gingerly slipping first my right, then my left foot slightly out of my shoes. When everyone else finally sat down I followed and flipped open the program.

Mr. Page started introductions. Then he asked the National Honor Society Students to stand for recognition and applause. After that, he announced scholarships. My feet were burning hot. I could feel them beginning to swell, but resisted the urge to bend over and rub them.

"You will notice a single asterisk next to one of the names in the Class of 1967. This graduating student is a correspondence student from Gold Creek."

I sat back in my chair and felt the heat from my feet travel to my face.

"Melody has been enrolled in the correspondence school program since the sixth grade when she started Calvert Courses. She then continued onward to complete four years of high school through the

University of Nebraska Correspondence Division. Melody accepted our invitation to be here tonight to participate in the graduation ceremony. I would like both Melody and her parents to stand now and receive the welcome and recognition due this entire family. This night many of us can share in their personal accomplishment."

The student next to me nudged my ribs. I rose slowly, turning ever so slightly to face the auditorium of people behind me. Mom and Dad were standing too. I sat down before the applause stopped and looked straight ahead at the stage. There were three stairs between me and the stack of diplomas on the table where Mr. Page stood. As I negotiated them a few minutes later I knew Mom and Dad were holding their breath right along with me. Finally, hands shaken, and tassel turned, I held the red–padded folder tightly. Then after a quick recessional, and still in my cap and gown, I searched the reception area for Mom and Dad.

"I did it. I really did it, didn't I!" I gave them both a hug.

"There you are." One of the graduates, already out of her gown, grabbed my elbow. "You'd better hurry and change. You're due at the Valedictorian's house for a dance and reception."

"Can I go?" I looked at my parents.

"You've got to go," the student said. "You're the Guest of Honor."

I paused, wanting to show Mom and Dad my diploma. But suddenly it wasn't the time or place.

"Go on. Get out of here and have a good time. We'll see you later at the motel," Dad said.

I slipped out of my gown and only then realized that I had no other way to carry my diploma than in my hand, so I held onto it throughout the night. It was really late when one of the parents drove me back to the motel, but Mom and Dad were still awake and waiting.

"Well, do you want to see it?" I held the folder outward.

"You bet we do." Mom received the diploma and sat on the edge of the bed with Dad.

I hovered around them as together they opened the folder. The top half had a screen print of Wasilla High School. The bottom half held a piece of paper we read and reread in silence.

"I told you I'd do it," I said as Dad put his arm around Mom.

"You did it, all right," Dad said. He closed the folder and handed it back to me. "And you know what else?" The corners of his mouth twitched upwards slightly.

"What?" I responded cautiously.

"You were the only one in step."

EPILOGUE

The branch of the river was low that fall, unlike the year when I'd flown back from my trip to Stephan Lake in the small noisy float plane. It had landed somewhere in the river nearby and taxied several hundred feet upstream to arrive at the first slough. Across the river and to my left, an island where we'd harvested spruce timber still held mature trees which would never feel the sting of a sawmill's blade. To my right, an ever-eroding high gravel bank loomed far above.

I studied the high water mark along the bank's edge, then continued my barefooted walk through the river shallows toward the mouth of the first slough.

It had been seven years since we'd come to this land and I'd first felt that same late August sun warm my back. I knew the mountain tundra wore its fall colors but hadn't had the chance to climb it and witness the transformation. Nor had there been time to till the field. We had managed to do other things that summer though. Mom had a shed full of wood to last the winter, an indoor bathroom, and a telephone. I could call her from college anytime I wanted. And I had the feeling I would do so very often.

An unmistakable splashing sound made me turn my attention from the eroding bank. I pulled my hair back and listened, then began rock-hopping several dozen yards upstream.

The salmon was wedged between several large boulders. His back and gills were above water and he used all his waning strength in futile attempts to return to the deeper current.

I wondered how far had he already come, this battered warrior with so much instinctive will. He'd come past the fishing trollers in the ocean with their unmerciful nets; past Native fish wheels working throughout daylit summer nights to dredge him from the cold Alaskan river water; past the sports fishermen, homesteaders, and bears which had left a ragged scar of a missed meal on the salmon's broad side.

EPILOGUE

I reached down and stroked my hand over the scarred scales. Then I picked up the salmon, walked a few feet to the main stream and placed the fish in the deep murky current. His red hump disappeared below the surface of gray, glacial water.

I wondered where he was headed. To the first slough? Had one of his kin been my dinner? Maybe he was off to some stream yet to be explored, a stream where he'd live his last few days of satisfied old age in peace.

At that moment I was certain of only two things. He was headed upstream, and he wouldn't be back.

THE END

Whatever Happened To ...

Melody, Sandy and Gay at a recent get together in Anchorage.

After publishing my first book, *Growing Up at Gold Creek – The Gonna People* in 1979, I received many inquiries about when the sequel, which I'd hinted at, would be forthcoming. There was a ten-year lapse between that first book, which told of our first winter's experiences at Gold Creek, and this one. For those readers who have expressed an interest in this homestead drama, another ten-year wait to find out what happened after I left the homestead is not necessary.

Instead, I submit the following abridged sequel to the sequel.

My brother went to Viet Nam and returned to Alaska safely. He worked on the pipeline as a heavy equipment mechanic and operator. He remained stubborn up until his death in 1977 at age 28 while attempting to pilot a small single-engine aircraft in minimum visibility conditions from Barter Island in northernmost Alaska, back to Fairbanks. Our family reconciled our differences not long after that. My first book was dedicated to his memory.

Gay, Sandra, and Dad all live in Anchorage. Gay returned to Alaska from New York in 1968, with her husband. She lives in Anchorage, has four children, and is currently pursuing a college degree. Gay's talent as an artist is demonstrated in the homestead map found in this book.

Sandra has three children, three grandchildren, and has remarried. In 1986 she published her own version of our first year's experiences at Gold Creek in a book titled *This Distant Land*.

WHATEVER HAPPENED TO...

Alice and Leon worked at Curry Mess Hall as innkeepers in the late 1970's and early 1980's.

Between the time I left the homestead and the early 1980's, both Dad and Mom worked for, and retired from, the railroad. During those years they lived off and on at the homestead and at Curry, Alaska, 16 miles south of Gold Creek, where they were innkeepers for the railroad at the Curry mess hall. The mess hall, like the Gold Creek railroad section house, has since been demolished by the railroad. Later, Dad and Mom lived in Anchorage where they moved in the early 1980's due to a chronic illness Mom had developed. She passed away December, 1984. Dad has since remarried.

The parkas were made in 1970. Mrs. Ihly lives at the Pioneer Home in Anchorage. Doug and Mr. Andrews have passed away. Bob lives in Anchorage with his wife and two children. I have lost track of the other characters.

The homestead is still owned by Dad. Years of natural reclamation have turned it back to a rustic state. The house collapsed in the spring of 1985. My last physical visit was in 1982, but my childhood spirit remains there to this day.

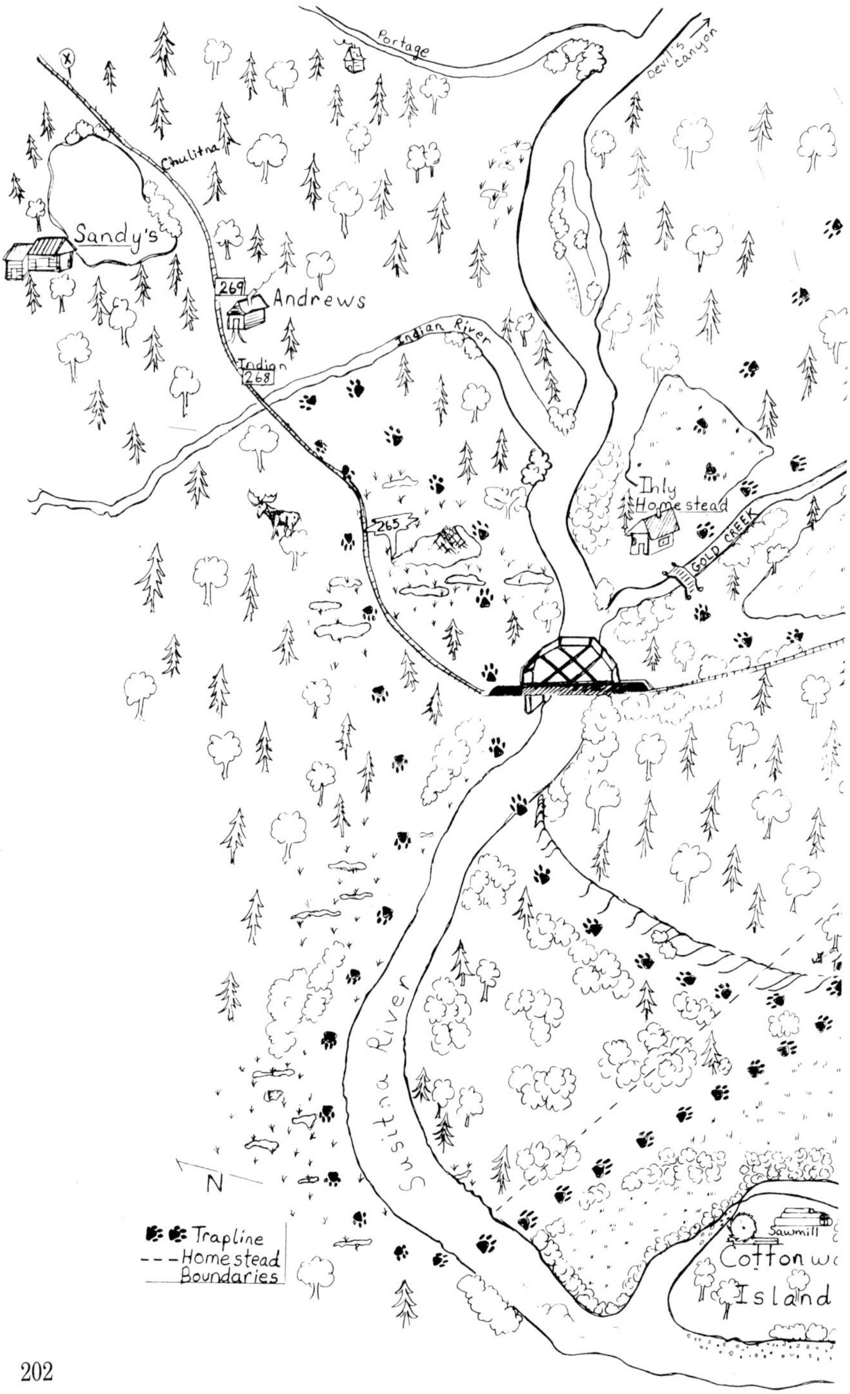
Portage
Devil's canyon
Chulitna
Sandy's
269
Andrews
Indian
268
Indian River
Ihly
Homestead
GOLD CREEK
265
Susitna River
N
Trapline
Homestead Boundaries
Sawmill
Cottonw
Island

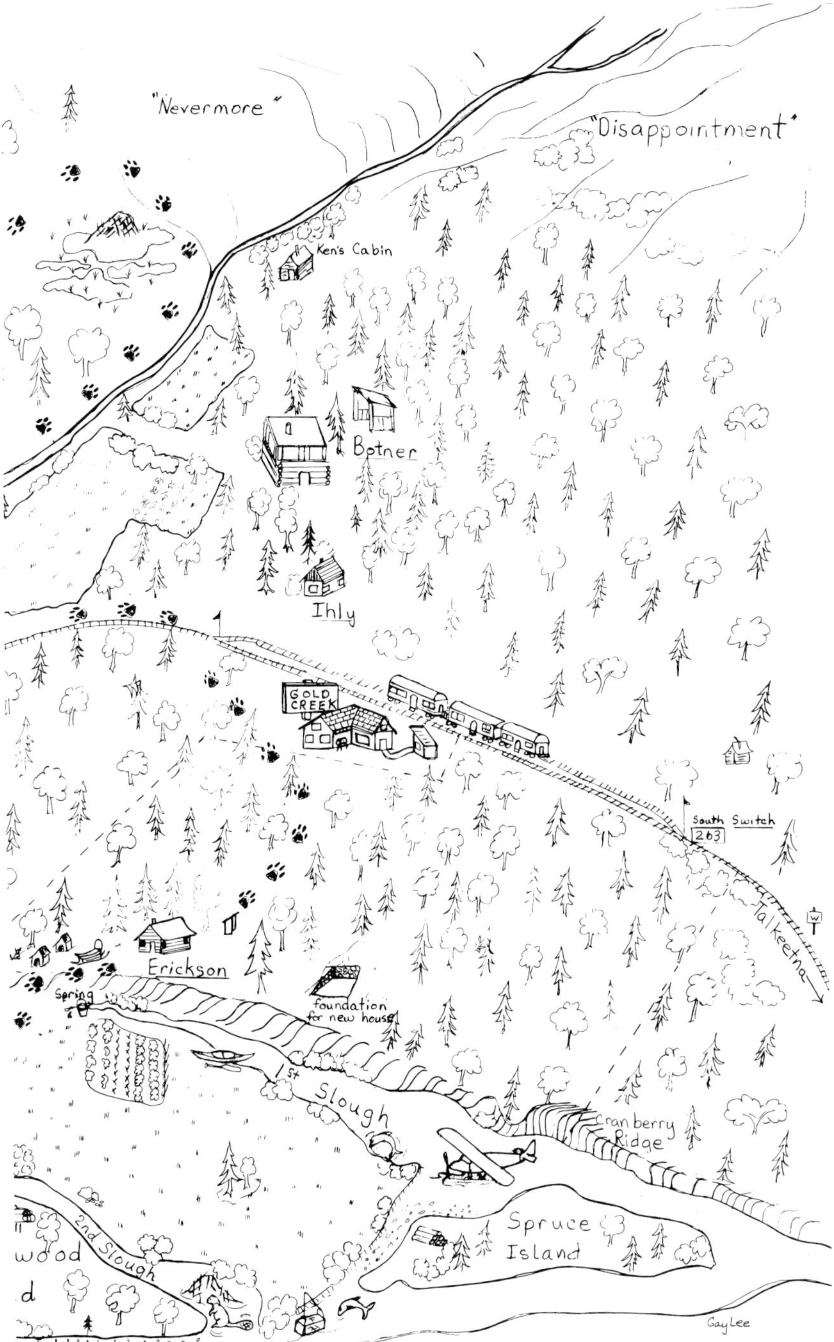
"Nevermore"
"Disappointment"
Ken's Cabin
Botner
Ihly
GOLD CREEK
South Switch
263
Talkeetna
Erickson
Spring
foundation for new house
1st Slough
Cranberry Ridge
Spruce Island
2nd Slough
GayLee

The photos on this page are the only ones that survived the cabin fire of 1964.

Back of the cabin. Snow was packed down by snowshoe the night before so window could be seen. 1962

Spook, Melody, John and Gay pose with martin, wolverine and beaver on stretching boards. A hind quarter of moose is hanging from the meat rack behind Melody. 1962

The family's first building project was the 'chalet.' Built in 1962, it was used as a storage cabin for anything that didn't fit in the 12 x 20 cabin in which they lived.

The Gold Creek section house, which has since been torn down.

Ren, the family 'bird dog' poses in front of the Big Susitna River Bridge.

John with a caribou bagged during a Labor Day hunt on Nevermore mountain. 1964

Bob Wilder poses with part of the Erickson family in front of the old cabin the October before it burned down. From left, Bob, Dad, Gay, John and Melody.

The cat and cabin from the north side. The framework of logs began as an expansion to the old cabin, but actually became the new house.

John, Gay and Dad — the day after the cabin burned down. December 1964

Melody scrutinizes a high school correspondence course syllabus at Botner's house. 1966

John, Melody (with Ren) and Ken at Botner's Sawmill on Cottonwood Island. 1965

The new house was built at the old cabin location. It was constructed with spruce logs and cottonwood lumber from the Erickson homestead. 1965 – 1966

The author with some of the furs the family trapped over six winters.

The only bear ever shot by the homestead family was a black bear that insisted on raiding their garbage pit. The subsequent rug was put to use in Melody's room in the new house.

John in Anchorage, just before leaving for Viet Nam. 1967

Melody and fellow graduate Kathy Clyde at high school graduation in Wasilla. 1967

In March 1976 an ice jam on the Big Susitna River below the bridge made the river jump its banks. Most of the 20 acres of cleared land on the Erickson homestead was stripped bare of soil.